Social Studies Curriculum Planning Resources

A publication of
National Council for
the Social Studies

 **KENDALL/HUNT PUBLISHING COMPANY**
2460 Kerper Boulevard P.O. Box 539 Dubuque, Iowa 52004-0539

National Council for the Social Studies

President
C. Frederick Risinger
Indiana University
Bloomington, Indiana

President-Elect
Margit McGuire
Seattle University
Seattle, Washington

Vice President
Charlotte C. Anderson
Education for Global Involvement
Northeastern Illinois University
Chicago, Illinois

Executive Director
Frances Haley

Board of Directors
Susan A. Adler
Richard Diem
Emma Flood
Jesus Garcia
Lesley M. Handley
H. Michael Hartoonian
Tedd Levy
Mary McFarland
Pat Nickell
Paul H. Pangrace
Gail Riley
Angie Rinaldo
Patricia King Robeson
Donald O. Schneider
Rick Theisen
Judith Wooster
Michael Young

Ex Officio
Christine Allen (Steering Committee)

Director of Publications
Salvatore J. Natoli

Publications Committee
Virginia Atwood, Chair
David A. Welton, Vice Chair
Charles E. Holt
John A. Rossi
Charles F. Smith, Jr.
Michael Solliday
Anne H. Stoddard
Mary Jane Turner
John Weakland
Angie Rinaldo, Board Liaison

Ex Officio
Charlotte C. Anderson
Frances Haley
Salvatore J. Natoli, Editor, *Social Education*
Huber Walsh, Editor, *Social Studies and the Young Learner*
Millard Clements, Editor, *Theory and Research in Social Education*

Editorial Staff on this publication:

Frances Haley, Executive Director, NCSS
Salvatore Natoli, Director of Publications, NCSS
Pamela Hollar, Associate Editor, NCSS

Layout and design: Dan Kaufman, Coordinator of Desktop Publishing, NCSS

Library of Congress Catalog Card Number: 90-63206

ISBN 0-8403-6379-6

Copyright© 1990 by National Council for the Social Studies.
All rights reserved. **Teachers may reproduce material from this book for classroom use only.** Under all other circumstances, no part of this book may be reproduced, stored in a retrieval system, or transmitted, in any form or by any means, electronic, mechanical, photocopying, recording, or otherwise, without the prior written permission of the copyright owner.

Printed in the United States of America
10 9 8 7 6 5 4 3 2

Table of Contents

Foreword 1
Introduction 2

NCSS Curriculum Statements 7
NCSS Essentials of Social Studies 9
NCSS Social Studies Curriculum Guidelines 12
Scope and Sequence Criteria 16

NCSS-Endorsed Social Studies Scopes and Sequences 17
Social Studies for Citizens of a Strong and Free Nation 19
Social Studies Themes and Questions to Reflect Principles and Practices in a Democracy 38
Social Studies within a Global Education 60

NCSS Position Statements and Guidelines 71
Social Studies for Early Childhood and Elementary School Children Preparing for the
    21st Century 73
Essential Characteristics of a Citizenship Education Program 87
Essential Characteristics of a Citizenship Program: Criteria Checklist 88
Global Education 89
Study About Religions in the Social Studies Curriculum 92
Teaching about Science, Technology and Society in Social Studies: Education for
    Citizenship in the 21st Century 94

Curriculum Documents in ERIC: A Select Annotated Bibliography for
Social Studies Educators 107

Foreword

Frances Haley

National Council for the Social Studies has a variety of resources for social studies professionals to use in planning, evaluating, and revising the social studies program. Those resources are presented in this collection along with an annotated bibliography of resources produced by other organizations and publishers.

In the Introduction, Mary McFarland presents a list of "curriculum constants"—the knowledge, skills, attitudes, and actions that are essential for any social studies curriculum. She also poses a set of questions that should be used to review and evaluate the social studies curriculum.

Section II presents three NCSS statements that encapsulate criteria for excellence in social studies. The first is criteria that should be addressed by any social studies curriculum scope and sequence design. The Essentials of Social Studies outlines essentials for a professionally designed scope and sequence and lists knowledge, democratic beliefs, thinking skills, participation skills, and civic action that should be present in exemplary programs. The third document details the NCSS Social Studies Curriculum Guidelines in outline form.

Three model scope and sequence statements, which most closely meet the criteria detailed in Section II, are presented fully in the third section. "Social Studies for Citizens of a Strong and Free Nation" is a scope and sequence based on social studies' mandate to provide citizenship education. The authors state: "That mandate is to provide every American school child and adolescent with the opportunity to learn the knowledge, the abilities and skills, and the beliefs and values needed for competent participation in social, political, and economic life. "Social Studies Themes and Questions to Reflect Principles and Practices in a Democracy" is a thematic approach to scope and sequence, "based upon a series of necessary (though not sufficient) themes and questions that can initiate a dialogue about the logical, philosophical, and psychological relevance of scope and sequence (ideals) to the teaching, learning, and context of social studies instruction (practice)" in a democracy. The third model, "Social Studies Within a Global Education" espouses a global approach to the social studies curriculum, extending "the view of citizenship since, in today's world, citizenship increasingly includes participation not only in the community, state, and nation but in the global community as well." It is based on the belief that "the scope of the social studies curriculum should reflect the present and historical realities of a global society."

Section IV contains NCSS position statements and guidelines that affect social studies curriculum. Guidelines on citizenship; elementary/early childhood education; global education; study about religions; and science, technology, and society are included.

The final section is an annotated bibliography prepared by John Patrick and C. Frederick Risinger of the ERIC Clearinghouse for Social Studies/Social Science Education. They have annotated recent reports and curriculum guidelines for social studies prepared by school districts, state departments of education, and organizations throughout the United States. The authors have included detailed information on how to locate these documents.

As you begin to evaluate and revise the social studies curriculum, we hope that these documents, prepared by thoughtful, concerned social studies professionals and endorsed by National Council for the Social Studies, will assist you in your efforts. We believe this document serves the goals of NCSS:

- to provide leadership in the field of social studies education;
- to provide professional development for social studies educators; and
- to foster and strengthen the advancement of social studies education.

Frances Haley is Executive Director, National Council for the Social Studies.

Introduction

Mary McFarland

Social studies curriculum planning—designing coherent, cumulative learning experiences for students—is one of the most significant activities a social studies professional will ever undertake; but it also carries its own special challenges. Whether the plan is for the nation, the state, local, or district level, or for a specific social studies course or grade level, it is strengthened by considering as wide a range of possibilities and options as possible.

Exciting change and potential are the major characteristics of today's "social studies world." Many of us are privileged to witness and often participate in the development of scope and sequence options—some developed within the nation's largest social studies professional organization, NCSS, some as commission reports, some as state proposals, and many as local district initiatives. *Social Studies Curriculum Planning Resources* can provide curriculum planners with many valuable resources that represent a wide range of the available options that should be considered. The document also includes many other important resources in the annotated bibliography.

NCSS believes that this special professional activity—planning what is of worth and value for students to study and how it shall be organized and presented—demands and, in fact, begins with an examination of the purpose of social studies education. The questions of what and how always follow the much more fundamental question of why: Why do we think social studies education is a basic for all students in a democratic republic?

All of the NCSS documents in this packet, as well as materials referenced in the bibliography, address the question of why and, surprisingly, there is more harmony than one might suspect among the options and models—harmony in the form of "curriculum constants" or strands that should be embedded in the curriculum at all levels. In addition, it is obvious that the various developers of materials and referenced resources in this packet also answer many of the same key questions inherent in the challenge of curriculum planning. As you review the packet materials and other suggested references, you will undoubtedly discover additional curriculum constants and key questions of special importance as you plan social studies curricula to address the needs of your own students, now and into the future.

NCSS and the Question of *Why*

NCSS has recognized since its founding that citizenship education is a central goal of the social studies. A basic purpose for K-12 social studies education is to provide educational experiences that prepare students to hold "the office of citizen"—the only role in society that bonds every person in our nation to every other, regardless of gender, race, ethnicity, sexual orientation, status, or ability. Public education was founded to accomplish citizenship education and has taken as its goal the education of all citizens. The future of this young and fragile experiment—a democratic republic based on participatory citizenship—depends heavily upon thoughtful, systematic, regular, and engaging instruction that models democratic climate in K-12 social studies classes.

Social studies education received federal support in the 1960s and '70s for national curriculum projects which attempted to make available (especially to secondary students) rigorous knowledge, processes, and habits of mind from history, geography, sociology, anthropology, psychology, economics and political science. Scholars who were involved in those projects believe today that their influence would have been more pervasive had classroom teachers been more integrally involved in the actual development of the projects, rather than merely expected to accept and implement them. Yet many of the concepts and processes promoted in these projects have found their way into classrooms in the form of improved materials and teaching strategies. The lesson from this earlier, intensive era of reform appears to be supported as a tenet of one of today's most respected educational reformers: involve professionals in curriculum planning and encourage them to apply their own professional intelligence in thinking through how to best meet the needs of their students (Sizer 1985). We encourage social studies educators to examine, discuss, and thoughtfully decide which curriculum option, combination of options, or creative new option can best address the needs of K-12 social studies students.

Curriculum Options

Beginning in the earliest primary classrooms, the elementary program establishes a strong foundation for learning at the secondary levels. Information from surveys, case studies, and literature reviews in the late '70s and early '80s indicate a nationwide similarity, persistent for more than seventy years, in topics and courses taught in K-12 social studies across the nation, with the most widespread designation as follows (*Social Education*, May 1980):

K—Self, School, Community, Home
1—Families
2—Neighborhoods
3—Communities
4—State History, Geographic Regions
5—United States History
6—World Cultures, Western Hemisphere
7—World Geography or History
8—American History
9—Civics or World Cultures
10—World History
11—American History
12—American Government

Of course there has been and is variance from this pattern. While some curriculum patterns emphasize one discipline, others include concepts from many disciplines—history, geography, anthropology, sociology, political science, economics, psychology; others focus on interdisciplinary learning. More recently, social studies educators have become increasingly aware of the potential benefits of community service to civic education at all levels, especially as students are actively engaged in planning, implementing, discussing, and evaluating the specific civic benefits of their involvement (*Social Education*, October 1989).

Within the last five years, several additional scope and sequence options have been put forward at the national and state levels. Options have been developed by the National Council for the Social Studies (*Social Education*, April 1984; November/December 1986; October 1989); by the National Commission on Social Studies in the Schools (November 1989); and by several states. Regardless of the developer, major concerns of the field are reflected in curriculum constants—the types of knowledge, skills, attitudes, and civic action/social participation that all of these K-12 options embrace.

Curriculum Constants

Certain curriculum constants or curriculum strands appear across many of the currently recommended options as crucial for inclusion in the K-12 social studies program. A few examples are presented below. You may wish to add your own curriculum constants.

Citizen Knowledge

- Knowledge of our nation's historic, geographic, social, cultural, economic, and political roots and the ability to compare and contrast this knowledge as it applies to other nations of the world
- Knowledge of the development of our nation's value system with its balance between a core of shared civic values and its respect for diversity

- Knowledge of the development of other value systems among civilizations and nations of the world across time and space
- Knowledge of the relationship of the historic past and dynamic present to serve as the basis for an improved future

Citizen Skills

- Logical and creative thinking as well as the ability to communicate ideas clearly in spoken and written form
- Civic participation skills which include the ability to reflect, research, and discuss in order to understand important issues and to plan positive civic responses aimed at enhancing the common good

Citizen Attitudes

- Commitment to basic civic values
- Respect for diversity
- Commitment to being a positive influence and making a positive contribution

Citizen Actions

- Applying social studies knowledge, skills, and attitudes to alleviate or resolve issues and problems in the classroom, school, community, nation, and the world

Key Questions To Ask of the K-12 Social Studies Program for the '90s and Beyond

As you work to plan and strengthen social studies instruction in your schools, consider the key questions listed below. Be sure to add your own.

1. Is the K-12 program (or this specific course) designed with clear purpose(s) to ensure important, cumulative learning?
2. Is sufficient instructional time available to accomplish the purpose(s)?
3. Within the K-12 curriculum is enough coverage provided to establish the context for several in-depth studies of highly significant issues, topics, or events? Has an appropriate balance been established between coverage (to assure sufficient context for comprehension) and depth (to assure interest and meaning)?
4. Does the content include a balance among the past and present and the application of imagination to the future, so that students recognize the link between social studies learning and real life and its improvement?
5. Is there appropriate attention to a balance of local, national, and international content and recognition of the interrelationship among these contexts?
6. Is the content based on history, geography, and the social sciences (e.g., psychology, sociology, economics, anthropology, political science) as well as integration with other natural allies such as literature, the arts, science, composition, and speech?
7. Are a variety of materials available; e.g., textbooks, visuals, related fact and fiction, news sources, primary sources?
8. Are a variety of strategies implicit; e.g., cooperative learning, discussions, simulations, research projects, community service?
9. Are a variety of types of evaluations possible; e.g., projects, service, exhibitions, portfolio collections?
10. Do classroom and school climate model democracy and promote participatory citizenship?

11. Do the social studies professionals recognize social studies as the cornerstone of preparation for each student to assume with competence the office of citizen?
12. Will each student gain knowledge of their heritage and develop a hopeful and powerful vision of her or his own personal importance to the improvement of the common good within the immediate local community and beyond?
13. Is each student encouraged to make a positive contribution in her or his current and future spheres of influence—the classroom, the school, the community, the nation, and the world?

Summary

Professional participation is essential in thoughtfully planning curriculum to address the '90s and beyond. NCSS recognizes that there are many valid approaches to social studies curriculum planning and many valid curriculum models to prepare students for the office of citizen. We sincerely hope that the materials in this NCSS Curriculum Planning Packet will assist you in planning exemplary K-12 social studies programs. Curriculum planning in the social studies is a special opportunity with its own set of special challenges. In a "we the people" democratic republic, it also carries its own urgency and its own set of rewards when it leads students to become informed, caring, participating citizens.

Mary McFarland was President of National Council for the Social Studies, 1989-1990. She is Instructional Coordinator of Social Studies K-12 and Director of Staff Development at Parkway School District, St. Louis, Mo.

References

"Feature: Three Scope and Sequence Alternatives." *Social Education* 53 (October 1989): 375-403. National Council for the Social Studies, Washington, D.C.

Report of the Curriculum Task Force of the National Commission on Social Studies in the Schools. Washington, D.C.: National Commission on Social Studies in the Schools, 1989.

"Scope and Sequence Alternatives for Social Studies." *Social Education* 50 (November/December 1986): 484-485.

Sizer, Theodore R. *Horace's Compromise: The Dilemma of the American High School.* Boston: Houghton Mifflin Company, 1985.

"Task Force on Scope and Sequence." *Social Education* 48 (April 1984): 249-261.

NCSS
Curriculum Statements

NCSS Essentials of Social Studies 9
NCSS Social Studies Curriculum Guidelines 12
Scope and Sequence Criteria 16

NCSS Essentials of Social Studies

POSITION STATEMENT & GUIDELINES

Citizen participation in public life is essential to the health of our democratic system. Effective social studies programs help prepare young people who can identify, understand, and work to solve the problems that face our increasingly diverse nation and interdependent world. Organized according to a professionally designed scope and sequence, such programs

1. begin in pre-school and continue throughout formal education and include a range of related electives at the secondary level;
2. foster individual and cultural identity;
3. include observation of and participation in the school and community as part of the curriculum;
4. deal with critical issues and the world as it really is;
5. prepare students to make decisions based on American principles;
6. demand high standards of performance and measure student success by means that require more than the memorization of information;
7. depend on innovative teachers, broadly prepared in history, the humanities, the social sciences, educational theory and practice;
8. involve community members as resources for program development and student involvement; and
9. lead to citizenship participation in public affairs.

In 1979, National Council for the Social Studies joined with eleven other professional associations to reaffirm the value of a balanced education.* We now enumerate the essentials of exemplary social studies programs. Such programs contribute not only to the development of students' capacity to read and compute, but also link knowledge and skills with an understanding of and commitment to democratic principles and their application.

Knowledge

Students need knowledge of the world at large and the world at hand, the world of individuals and the world of institutions, the world past, the world present and future. An exemplary social studies curriculum links information presented in the classroom with experiences gained by students through social and civic observation, analysis, and participation.

Classroom instruction that relates content to information drawn from the media and from experience focuses on the following areas of knowledge:

- History and culture of our nation and the world.
- Geography—physical, political, cultural, and economic.
- Economics—theories, systems, structures, and processes.
- Social institutions—the individual, the group, the community, and the society.
- Intergroup and interpersonal relationships.
- World-wide relationships of all sorts between and among nations, races, cultures, and institutions.

From this knowledge base, exemplary programs teach skills, concepts, and generalizations that can help students understand the sweep of human affairs and ways of managing conflict consistent with democratic procedures.

Democratic Beliefs

Fundamental beliefs drawn from the Declaration of Independence and the United States Constitution with its Bill of Rights form the basic principles of our democratic constitutional order. Exemplary school programs do not indoctrinate students to accept these ideas blindly, but present knowledge about their historical derivation and contemporary application essential to understanding our society and its institutions. Not only should such ideas be discussed as they relate to the curriculum and to current affairs, they should also be mirrored by teachers in their classrooms and embodied in the school's daily operations.

These democratic beliefs depend upon such practices as due process, equal protection, and civic participation, and are rooted in the concepts of:

- Justice
- Responsibility
- Diversity
- Equality
- Freedom
- Privacy

Thinking Skills

It is important that students connect knowledge with beliefs and action. To do that, thinking skills can be developed through constant systematic practice throughout the years of formal schooling. Fundamental to the goals of social studies education are those skills which help assure rational behavior in social settings.

In addition to strengthening reading and computation, there is a wide variety of thinking skills essential to the social studies which can be grouped into four major categories:

- Data-Gathering Skills. Learning to:
  Acquire information by observation
  Locate information from a variety of sources
  Compile, organize, and evaluate information
  Extract and interpret information
  Communicate orally and in writing
- Intellectual Skills. Learning to:
  Compare things, ideas, events, and situations on the basis of similarities and differences
  Classify or group items in categories
  Ask appropriate and searching questions
  Draw conclusions or inferences from evidence
  Arrive at general ideas
  Make sensible predictions from generalizations
- Decision-Making Skills. Learning to:
  Consider alternative solutions
  Consider the consequences of each solution
  Make decisions and justify them in relationship to democratic principles
  Act, based on those decisions
- Interpersonal Skills. Learning to:
  See things from the point of view of others
  Understand one's own beliefs, feelings, abilities, and shortcomings and how they affect relations with others
  Use group generalizations without stereotyping and arbitrarily classifying individuals
  Work effectively with others as a group member
  Give and receive constructive criticism
  Accept responsibility and respect the rights and property of others

Participation Skills

As a civic participant, the individual uses the knowledge, beliefs, and skills learned in the school, the social studies classroom, the community, and the family as the basis for action.

Connecting the classroom with the community provides many opportunities for students to learn the basic skills of participation, from observation to advocacy. To teach participation, social studies programs need to emphasize the following kinds of skills:
- Work effectively in groups—organizing, planning, making decisions, taking action
- Form coalitions of interest with other groups
- Persuade, compromise, bargain
- Practice patience and perseverance in working for one's goal
- Develop experience in cross-cultural situations

Civic Action

Social studies programs that combine the acquisition of knowledge and skills with an understanding of the application of democratic beliefs to life through practice at social participation represent an ideal professional standard. Working to achieve that ideal is vital to the future of our society. However, even if excellent programs of social studies education were in place, there would often remain a missing element—the will to take part in public affairs. Formal education led by creative and humane teachers can provide the knowledge, the tools, the commitment for a thoughtful consideration of issues, and can even stimulate the desire to be active. But to achieve full participation, our diverse society must value and model involvement to emphasize for young people the merit of taking part in public life.

During the period of the bicentennial of our Constitution and Bill of Rights, is it not time for us to recommit ourselves as a nation to strong education for civic responsibility?

* Essentials of Education Statement, Washington, D.C. 1980

NCSS Social Studies Curriculum Guidelines

1. *The Social Studies Program Should Be Directly Related to the Age, Maturity, and Concerns of Students.*

POSITION STATEMENT & GUIDELINES

   1.1 Students should be involved in the formulation of goals, the selection of activities and instructional strategies, and the assessment of curricular outcomes.
   1.2 The school and its teachers should make steady efforts, through regularized channels and practices, to identify areas of concern to students.
   1.3 Students should have some choices, some options, within programs fitted to their needs, their concerns, and their social world.
   1.4 Students should have a social studies experience at all grade levels, K-12.
   1.5 The program should take into account the aptitudes, developmental capabilities, and psychological needs of the students.

2. *The Social Studies Program Should Deal with the Real Social World.*

   2.1 The program should focus on the social world as it is, its flaws, its strengths, its dangers, and its promise.
   2.2 The program should emphasize pervasive and enduring social issues.
   2.3 The program should demonstrate the relationships between the local and global aspects of social issues.
   2.4 The program should include analysis and attempts to formulate potential resolutions of present and controversial global problems such as racism, sexism, homophobia, world resources, nuclear proliferation, and ecological imbalance.
   2.5 The program should provide intensive and recurring cross-cultural study of groups to which students themselves belong and those to which they do not.
   2.6 The program should offer opportunities for students to meet, discuss, study, and work with members of racial, ethnic, and national groups other than their own.
   2.7 The program should build upon realities of the immediate school community.
   2.8 Participation in the real social world, both in school and out, should be considered a part of the social studies program.
   2.9 The program should provide the opportunity for students to examine potential future conditions and problems.

3. *The Social Studies Program Should Draw from Currently Valid Knowledge Representative of Human Experience, Culture, and Beliefs.*

   3.1 The program should emphasize currently valid concepts, principles, and theories in history and the social sciences.
   3.2 The program should develop proficiency in methods of inquiry in history and the social sciences and in techniques for processing social data.
   3.3 The program should develop students' ability to distinguish among empirical, logical, definitional, and normative propositions and problems.
   3.4 The program should draw upon history and all of the social sciences—anthropology, economics, geography, political science, sociology, and psychology.
   3.5 The program should draw from other related fields such as law, the humanities, the natural and applied sciences, and religion.

3.6 The program should represent some balance between the immediate social environment of students and the larger social world; between small group and public issues; among local, national, and global affairs; among past, present, and future directions; among Western and non-Western cultures; and among economically developed and developing nations.

3.7 The program should include the study not only of human achievements, but also of human failures.

4. Objectives Should Be Thoughtfully Selected and Clearly Stated in Such Form as to Furnish Direction to the Program.

4.1 Objectives should be carefully selected and formulated in the light of what is known about the students, their community, the real social world, and the fields of knowledge.

4.2 Knowledge, abilities, valuing, and social participation should all be represented in the stated objectives of social studies programs.

4.3 General statements of basic and long range goals should be translated into more specific objectives conceived in terms of behavior and content.

4.4 Classroom instruction should rely upon statements which identify clearly what students are to learn; learning activities and instructional materials should be appropriate for achieving the stated objectives.

4.5 Classroom instruction should enable students to see their goals clearly in what is to be learned, whether in brief instructional sequences or lengthy units of study.

4.6 Instructional objectives should develop all aspects of the affective, cognitive, and psychomotor domains.

4.7 Objectives should be reconsidered and revised periodically.

5. Learning Activities Should Engage the Student Directly and Actively in the Learning Process.

5.1 Students should have a wide and rich range of learning activities appropriate to the objectives of their social studies program.

5.2 Activities should include formulating hypotheses and testing them by gathering and analyzing data.

5.3 Activities should include using knowledge, examining values, communicating with others, and making decisions about social and civic affairs.

5.4 Students should be encouraged to become active participants in activities within their own communities.

5.5 Learning activities should be sufficiently varied and flexible to appeal to many kinds of students.

5.6 Activities should contribute to the students' perception of teachers as fellow inquirers.

5.7 Activities must be carried on in a climate which supports students' self-respect and opens opportunities to all.

5.8 Activities should stimulate students to investigate and to respond to the human condition in the contemporary world.

5.9 Activities that examine values, attitudes, and beliefs should be undertaken in an environment that respects each student's right to privacy.

6. ***Strategies of Instruction and Learning Activities Should Rely on a Broad Range of Learning Resources.***

   6.1 A social studies program requires a great wealth of appropriate instructional resources; no one textbook can be sufficient.

   6.2 Printed materials must accommodate a wide range of reading abilities and interests, meet the requirements of learning activities, and include many kinds of material from primary as well as secondary sources, from social science and history as well as the humanities and related fields, from other nations and cultures as well as our own, and from current as well as basic sources.

   6.3 A variety of media should be available for learning through seeing, hearing, touching, and acting, and calling for thought and feeling.

   6.4 Social studies classrooms should draw upon the potential contributions of many kinds of resource persons and organizations representing many points of view, a variety of abilities, and a mix of cultures and nationalities.

   6.5 Classroom activities should use the school and community as a learning laboratory for gathering social data and for confronting knowledge and commitments in dealing with social problems.

   6.6 The social studies program should have available many kinds of work space to facilitate variation in the size of groups, the use of several kinds of media, and a diversity of tasks.

7. ***The Social Studies Program Must Facilitate the Organization of Experience.***

   7.1 Structure in the social studies program must help students organize their experiences to promote growth.

   7.2 Learning experiences should be organized in such manner that students will learn how to continue to learn.

   7.3 The program must enable students to relate their experiences in social studies to other areas of experience.

   7.4 The formal pattern of the program should offer choice and flexibility.

8. ***Evaluation Should Be Useful, Systematic, Comprehensive, and Valid for the Objectives of the Program.***

   8.1 Evaluation should be based primarily on the school's own statements of objectives as the criteria for effectiveness.

   8.2 Included in the evaluation process should be assessment of progress not only in knowledge, but in skills and abilities, including thinking, valuing, and social participation.

   8.3 Evaluation data should come from many sources, not merely from paper-and-pencil tests, including observations of what students do outside as well as inside the classroom.

   8.4 Regular, comprehensive, and continuous procedures should be developed for gathering evidence of significant growth in learning over time.

   8.5 Evaluation data should be used for planning curricular improvements.

   8.6 Evaluation data should offer students, teachers, and parents help in the course of learning and not merely at the conclusion of some marking period.

   8.7 Both students and teachers should be involved in the process of evaluation.

   8.8 Thoughtful and regular re-examination of the basic goals of the social studies curriculum should be an integral part of the evaluation program.

9. *Social Studies Education Should Receive Vigorous Support as a Vital and Responsible Part of the School Program.*

   9.1 Appropriate instructional materials, time, and facilities must be provided for social studies education.

   9.2 Teachers should not only be responsible but should be encouraged to try out and adapt for their own students promising innovations such as simulation, newer curricular plans, discovery, and actual social participation.

   9.3 Decisions about the basic purposes of social studies education in any school should be as clearly related to the needs of its immediate community as to those of society at large.

   9.4 Teachers should participate in active social studies curriculum committees with decision-making as well as advisory responsibilities.

   9.5 Teachers should participate regularly in activities which foster their professional competence in social studies education: in workshops, or in-service classes, or community affairs, or in reading, studying, and travel.

   9.6 Teachers and others concerned with social studies education in the schools should have competent consultants available.

   9.7 Teachers and schools should have and be able to rely upon a district-wide policy statement on academic freedom and professional responsibility.

   9.8 Social studies education should expect to receive active support from administrators, teachers, boards of education, and the community.

   9.9 A specific minimal block of time should be allocated for social studies instruction each week.

Reference

"Revision of the NCSS Social Studies Curriculum Guidelines." *Social Education* 43 (April 1979): 261-273.

Scope and Sequence Criteria

The following criteria were developed by the NCSS Ad Hoc Committee on Scope and Sequence. They are the basic criteria that should be addressed by any social studies scope and sequence design, and take into account three dimensions: scholarship in history, the social sciences, and related fields; the needs of our society in its local, national, and global settings, and the needs, interests, and developmental characteristics of students.

A social studies scope and sequence should:

1. state the purpose and rationale of the program;
2. be internally consistent with its stated purposes and rationale;
3. designate content at every grade level, K-12;
4. recognize that learning is cumulative;
5. reflect a balance of local, national, and global content;
6. reflect a balance of past, present, and future content;
7. provide for students' understanding of the structure and function of social, economic, and political institutions;
8. emphasize concepts and generalizations from history and the social sciences;
9. promote the integration of skills and knowledge;
10. promote the integration of content across subject areas;
11. promote the use of a variety of teaching methods and instructional materials;
12. foster active learning and social interaction;
13. reflect a clear commitment to democratic beliefs and values;
14. reflect a global perspective;
15. foster the knowledge and appreciation of cultural heritage;
16. foster the knowledge and the appreciation of diversity;
17. foster the building of self-esteem;
18. be consistent with current research pertaining to how children learn;
19. be consistent with current scholarship in the disciplines;
20. incorporate thinking skills and interpersonal skills at all levels;
21. stress the identification, understanding, and solution of local, national, and global problems;
22. provide many opportunities for students to learn and practice the basic skills of participation from observation to advocacy;
23. promote the transfer of knowledge and skills to life; and
24. have the potential to challenge and excite students.

Reference

"Report of the Ad Hoc Committee on Scope and Sequence, 1988." *Social Education* 53, no. 6 (1989): 375.

NCSS-Endorsed Social Studies Scopes and Sequences

Social Studies for Citizens of a Strong and Free Nation 19
Social Studies Themes and Questions to Reflect Principles and Practices in a Democracy 38
Social Studies within a Global Education 60

Social Studies for Citizens of a Strong and Free Nation

Report of the National Council for the Social Studies Task Force on Scope and Sequence

November 1, 1983
Revised July 1, 1989

Social Studies and the Education of Citizens

The collapse of Athenian democracy is a tragic and complex history. But important to its decline were demagogues whipping up emotional mob passions while respectable Athenians avoided the vulgarities of the mob, lamented the extremism of its leaders, and pursued their private lives—unmindful of Pericles' eloquent wisdom.
—John C. Livingston and Robert G. Thompson, *The Consent of the Governed*

Political systems based mainly on such values as individual freedom and citizen participation historically have not enjoyed lengthy tenures. Time erodes the idealism under which they were established. Gradually, private interests dominate decision making. Pressure groups and influence peddlers manipulate the system to their own selfish ends. Nonparticipation reduces opportunities for citizens to control and direct their own destinies insofar as these are affected by the political system. Is this also to be the fate of the United States of America with its more than 200-year history of democratic government?

Citizenship means that individuals are fully franchised as members of a political community. The rights, duties, responsibilities, and entitlements embodied in the franchise apply evenhandedly to those who have the abilities and skills needed to participate in the social and political life of the group. But what becomes of persons who do not acquire such abilities and skills? Moreover, can a society that assumes responsible citizen involvement in decision making survive if its members do not, will not, or cannot participate in such decision making? Who, then, is responsible for educating the young in the knowledge, abilities, skills, beliefs, and values associated with such participation?

In recent years, much attention has focused on pluralism in the American social system. But underlying the great diversity of ethnic origins, interests, goals, and beliefs, there exists a layer of basic values and expectations on which there is or ought to be general concurrence. It is this set of common core values and expectations that provides standards for behavior in American life. How do young people learn those values and expectations that characterize effective citizenship, and who is responsible for transmitting them to the young?

The answer to the foregoing questions is that all agencies and institutions that work with young people share the responsibility for citizenship education. This includes the home and family; the community; religious groups; clubs, such as scouting and 4H; the media, especially television; and the schools. To some extent, citizenship education is the central mission of the *entire* K-12 curriculum. Young citizens are taught to exercise good habits of personal health, to be concerned about the well-being of others, to appreciate beauty in the arts, to read and write, to be discriminating in their television viewing—all of which fall within the scope of the general school curriculum, but are hardly the exclusive province of social studies.

Social studies education has a specific mandate in regard to citizenship education. *That mandate is to provide every American school child and adolescent with the opportunity to learn the knowledge, the abilities and skills, and the beliefs and values needed for competent participation in social, political, and economic life.* Social studies education has historically had a special responsibility for attaining such educational goals as those that develop knowledge of the American heritage, the economic system, law and government, political processes, the history and geography of the world, world cultures, the Constitution and the Bill of Rights, and the principles and ideals of American democracy. The professional practice of the social studies teacher may be defined as familiarizing children and youth with the meaning and practice of democratic government, its institutions, its historic values, and its requirements within the framework of an interdependent world of many nations whose people are oftentimes committed to competing or even conflicting ideologies and philosophical orientations. Most of all, social studies should prepare young people to put into practice what they learn in school as they fulfill their obligations as citizens, deciding and acting responsibly when confronted by personal and social issues and problems.

In the Preamble to the Constitution of the United States, we read that its framers ordained and established that document "in order to form a more perfect Union, establish justice, ensure domestic tranquility, provide for the common defense, promote the general welfare, and secure the blessings of liberty to ourselves and our posterity...." If these goals, so eloquently stated by founders of this nation, are to endure, the Task Force believes that America must have a strong program of social studies education operating in all classrooms across the nation every day throughout each school year.

The original title of this document, "In Search of a Scope and Sequence for Social Studies," was chosen to suggest that this effort is only the beginning of a process that should be conducted on a continuing basis. This is in a real sense a "period document"; it organizes and suggests a K-12 social studies scope and sequence that is realistically possible to implement in most of the schools of the nation. Many of the ideas embodied in it were developed during the growth years of experimentation and innovation in social studies. The Task Force believes that this program will serve well the purpose of educating young citizens who will spend their adult lives in the global community of the next century.

Definition and Goals

Definition

Social studies education is a basic component of the K-12 curriculum that (1) derives its goals from the nature of citizenship in a democratic society that is closely linked to other nations and peoples of the world; (2) draws its content primarily from history, the social sciences, and, in some respects, from the humanities and science; (3) is taught in ways that reflect an awareness of the personal, social, and cultural experiences and developmental levels of learners; and (4) facilitates the transfer of what is learned in school to the out-of-school lives of students.

The foregoing definition embodies contemporary professional thinking regarding the nature and purposes of social studies. It clearly focuses the purposes of social studies on citizenship education and stresses the importance of application of school learning to everyday life. It recognizes the need to deal with social studies content from a global perspective. Although the definition identifies history, the social sciences, humanities, and science as major sources of subject matter, it does not make the study of these disciplines an end in itself. Finally, the definition invites attention to the personal dimension of social studies in calling for teaching procedures that link it to the backgrounds and developmental levels of learners.

Two curriculum publications of the National Council for the Social Studies ("Social Studies Curriculum Guidelines," 1971, 1979; and "Essentials of the Social Studies," 1981) do not explicitly define social studies, but the intended meaning can be understood from the rationale and statement of major goals contained in them.[1] The Task Force assumes that the goal statements in those publications remain valid and has incorporated ideas from them in the account that follows.

Goals

Social studies programs have a responsibility to prepare young people to identify, understand, and work to solve the problems that face our increasingly diverse nation and interdependent world. Over the past several decades, the professional consensus has been that such programs ought to include goals in the broad areas of knowledge, democratic values, and skills.[2] Programs that combine the acquisition of knowledge and skills with the application of democratic values to life through social participation present an ideal balance in social studies. It is essential that these major goals be viewed as equally important. The relationship among knowledge, values, and skills is one of mutual support.

I. Knowledge

Knowledge is derived from encounters students have with the subject matter of the social studies. Knowledge makes it possible for students to understand human affairs and the human condition. Knowledge provides a basis for values and beliefs and is the vehicle for the development of skills. To develop their storehouse of knowledge, students need good sources of information, along with the skills required for using them.

In spite of modern technology—or perhaps because of it—ordinary citizens have an enormous need for knowledge that is useful in making informed decisions. Information gained in the classroom should be helpful in understanding events and conditions in the world outside of school. *Information must also be linked with experiences encountered by students in their daily lives.* This can be accomplished in part through social and civic observation, analysis, participation, and community service. The following are essential sources of subject matter from which knowledge goals for social studies should be selected:

History—of the United States and the world; understanding change and learning to deal with it

Geography—physical, political, cultural, economic; worldwide relationships

Government—theories, systems, structures, processes

Law—civil, criminal, constitutional, international

Economics—theories, systems, structures, processes

Anthropology and Sociology—cultures, social institutions, the individual, the group, the community, the society

Psychology—the individual in intergroup and interpersonal relationships

Humanities—the literature, art, music, dance, and drama of cultures

Science—the effects of natural and physical science on human relationships

II. Democratic Values and Beliefs

Democratic values and beliefs constitute a second category of social studies goals. Values constitute the standards or criteria against which individual behavior and group behavior are judged. Beliefs represent commitments to those values.

The Declaration of Independence and the United States Constitution with its Bill of Rights set forth the basic principles of our democratic constitutional order. It is from these documents that our fundamental political values and concepts are derived. Social studies programs should not indoctrinate students to accept these ideas blindly, but should have students learn about their historical roots and show their contemporary application. Such ideas should be analyzed in context as they relate to the topics studied and to current affairs.

They should also be modeled by teachers in their classrooms and reflected in the school's daily operations.

Democratic processes include the practice of due process, equal protection, and civic participation; they are rooted in such values as:

Justice	Human dignity	Equality	Fairness
Responsibility	Integrity	Rule of law	Honesty
Freedom	Loyalty	Diversity	Authority
Privacy	International human rights		

III. Skills

Skill development is a third category of social studies goals. *A skill is defined as the ability to do something proficiently in repeated performances.* Skills are processes that enable students to link knowledge with beliefs that lead to action. Skills are developed through sequential systematic instruction and practice throughout the K-12 years. Skills essential to citizen participation in civic affairs can be grouped in a problem-solving or decision-making sequence in the following major categories:

Skills related to acquiring information
- Reading skills
- Study skills
- Reference and information-search skills
- Technical skills unique to the use of electronic devices

Skills related to organizing and using information
- Thinking skills
- Decision-making skills
- Metacognitive skills

Skills related to interpersonal relationships and social participation
- Personal skills
- Group interaction skills
- Social and political participation skills

A more complete list of skills is presented on pages 36-37; a list of beliefs and values is provided on pages 31 and 32.

Goals for social studies are targeted on educating citizens to become informed, to develop skills necessary for citizen participation in social, civic, and political processes, and to embrace the values and beliefs that characterize citizens in a democratic society. Democracy thrives on citizen involvement and constructive social criticism; therefore, social studies should leave students with a feeling of responsibility to involve themselves in social, civic, and political affairs; and with a sense of confidence that they can *make a difference* in resolving social conflicts and basic societal problems.

Defining Scope and Sequence

The term 'scope' refers to the range of substantive content, values, skills, and learner experiences to be included in the social studies program. It also involves identifying appropriate life-related problems in order to give students opportunities to apply knowledge, values, and skills. The scope may be defined narrowly as, for example, simply stating the specific subjects or skills to be taught—e.g., history, map reading, world geography. It may also be defined so comprehensively that it does not provide meaningful direction to teachers. For example, "Social studies includes all of the interpersonal and social life of children and youth." Ideally, scope should define the outer boundaries of subject matter, values, skills, and learner experiences to be included in the program.

If social studies education "derives its goals from the nature of a democratic society closely linked to other nations and peoples of the world," and "draws its content primarily from history, the social sciences, and, in some respects, from the humanities and science," as is stated in the foregoing definition, topics and subjects will be included that are familiar to most parents and teachers. It is probably not possible to study close, primary human relationships without including such institutions as the home and family. Nor is it possible to learn about the development of the nation without studying its history. If persons are to learn about the various cultures of the world, they would doubtless study geographic characteristics, history, lifeways, art, literature, and music. Thus, it is not fruitful to try to define the scope of social studies in terms of wholly new and unfamiliar topics or subject matter. The familiarity of topics or subjects, however, does not excuse teaching them in the same old ways. The challenge to teachers is to shape those studies in ways that lead to the achievement of major social studies goals. Most important, the social issues and problems related to each area of study or topic should be identified so that they can be used as the basis for the practice of informed decision making, a basic composite skill needed for the exercise of responsible citizenship.

Teachers and curriculum planners have to decide not only what goes into the social studies program but the order in which the components are to appear, i.e., their *sequence*. Presentation sequences should represent decisions based on the application of psychological principles of human development and of professional judgment. Generally speaking, topics that are spatially, temporally, or psychologically *close* to learners have traditionally appeared in the early grades. Although there are many exceptions, there has been a tendency, at least in the elementary grades, to arrange topics from the near-at-hand to the faraway; from the here-and-now to the past. This expanding-environment principle has been widely used in planning social studies sequences for the elementary school since the 1930s.

The Task Force does not recommend that a social studies sequence rely solely on the expanding-environment principle. The life space of today's children is greatly affected by modern methods of communication and transportation. Who would claim that the life space of a six-year-old is limited to the local environment when each evening the child may view television accounts of events *in progress* from anywhere in the world? Therefore, the social studies curriculum should not move sequentially from topics that are near-at-hand to those that are farther away for the purpose of expanding the environment. The purpose of extending content outward, away from a self-centric focus, is to illustrate how people and places interact; how people of different areas depend on one another; how people are part of interlocking networks that sustain the life of modern societies; and how people and places everywhere fit into a global human community. What young children see going on around them is being done in one way or another by human beings everywhere.

Complexity has been another commonly accepted rationale for arranging content in a particular sequence. Topics perceived as simple were placed earlier in the program than those thought to be more difficult. Experience has shown that it is probably not possible to develop a workable sequence based *solely* on the assumption of complexity of content. Topics per se are intrinsically neither simple nor complex. Their complexity is regulated by instructional variables: the concepts, relationships, and issues selected for study; the amount, quality and use of instructional materials; the pace of the presentation; and the depth of understanding expected. This is illustrated by the fact that first graders and Ph.D. candidates in sociology both study the family, though at different levels of analysis. Scope and sequence charts that show subject matter arranged sequentially over a span of grades according to presumed difficulty may create erroneous impressions about the complexity of content.

Most important to sequence is not *what* is taught but *how* it is taught. Developmental research suggests that as children's capabilities develop, particular types of learning activities are more suitable than others. For example, young children learn best through concrete experience, manipulation of materials, observation of their environment, and through the resolution of problems closely related to their everyday lives. Similarly, perspective-taking abilities can be developed in middle childhood (after around age 10) through practice. Role-playing, case studies, and stories about other people's viewpoints might be used to foster that development. In the middle school or junior high school, most students begin to be able to do *if-then* thinking, making this a good time to give them experience in hypothesizing about causal relationships and in considering likely consequences of alternatives in problem situations. Those abilities can be further enhanced in high school by giving secondary school students opportunities to determine relationships among abstract concepts and to analyze events with consideration of multiple causes and multiple effects.

Because learning concepts, skills, and values is cumulative, ideas should be initially introduced to young children as concrete and simple. They should then be continually reinforced and applied—extending, expanding, and illuminating in more depth, taking advantage of students' development. This progression is difficult to show on a chart, but it should be evident in course guides, teacher guides, and student materials. The point is that charts can show topics and initial introduction of topics. The continual expansion of learning is represented on our skills chart. A similar chart for conceptual development would picture a spiraling curriculum.

The Task Force is recommending a *holistic-interactive* approach to the selection and placement of content. That is, content at any grade level should be presented in ways that provide, insofar as possible, a comprehensive view of a complex whole. Topics may be regarded as part of an interacting network that often extends worldwide. People everywhere arrange themselves in social groups and engage in basic social processes. The earth is the home of human beings no matter where they live individually. Potentially, all human beings can share in the legacies derived from all cultures. Subject matter at all grade levels needs to be taught from a global perspective. This approach is *interactive* because everything relates to everything else; it is *holistic* because it casts events in their broadest social context.

Illustrative Scope and Sequence—Content

The illustrative scope and sequence that follows deals with only one dimension of the social studies program—namely, the substantive content or subject matter. It is around this subject matter that skills and values (elaborated in other sections of this report) are taught. The material is presented for illustrative purposes and should not be construed as a model or ideal program. Rather, it is intended to extend the outer boundaries of existing practice, without moving so far out as to make the document unusable. Local school district curriculum developers, teachers, and lay persons should find the examples useful as a guide in building their own programs.

The following assumptions and conditions apply to this section of the document and to the two sections that deal with values and skills. They should be considered thoughtfully by teachers at *all* grade levels as "givens" in the development of a scope and sequence for social studies.

1. Although the scope and sequence do not presume or promote a particular method of teaching, it is assumed that critical thinking is a major outcome of social studies; and, therefore, teaching procedures at all levels—K-12—will attend to the development of this essential skill. Accordingly, teachers should use procedures that require direct student intellectual involvement. This means greater use of such learning activities as discussion, small-group work, student presentations, debate, simulations,

brainstorming, and independent study. The juggling of content from one grade to another or the search for new subject matter will not respond to the continuing problem of learner disinterest in social studies. The scope and sequence can do little if anything to remedy the use of uninspired teaching procedures.

2. It is assumed that subject matter at all grade levels will reflect a global perspective.

3. It is assumed that all teachers—K-12—share responsibility for teaching, extending, and refining skills; this assumption rejects the idea that skills are taught in the elementary grades and are applied in the upper grades. Skills are both taught *and* applied at all grade levels.

4. It is assumed that teachers will be sensitive to the dual—and often contradictory—thrusts of social studies education in a democratic society; namely, *socialization* and *social criticism*. A degree of social cohesiveness is needed to allow society to function; yet, it must not be such as to repress necessary dissension, which on occasion may be unpleasant and not socially acceptable. The challenge to education in a democratic society is to steer a course that will ensure necessary socialization of citizens and, at the same time, foster that spark of social criticism that has kept the lamp of liberty ignited for more than two centuries.

5. Citizens today live in a world faced with emergent problems and issues of such magnitude that they haunt the human family and cry for solution. Some of these challenges relate to the effects of science on human life: nuclear issues, acid rain, environmental contamination, waste disposal, and use of resources. Others have to do with social and moral issues of modern life: extending human rights, terrorism, hunger and starvation, loneliness, racism, drug use, AIDS, poverty, poor health, and ethics in public life. Finally, the overwhelming issue of war threatens the existence of all the world's people.

   The social studies curriculum cannot, and indeed should not, provide a separate course dealing with each of the many social issues and problems that confront society. Yet these issues and problems are relevant to modern life and to social studies education. This means that the scope and sequence must be flexible enough in its selection of subject matter to allow the teacher to deal with these emerging topics within the existing curriculum framework. The scope and sequence proposed in this document allows and encourages such infusion because of its holistic emphasis. It is assumed that teachers will recognize the potential of this scope and sequence for the inclusion of and the infusion of emerging social issues in their social studies programs.

6. The learning environment is a critical part of the support system for good social studies programs. There is no substitute for cooperative learning strategies for the enhancement of social participation skills. Involvement in student government—at all levels—can provide excellent lessons in democratic processes. A learning environment that respects diversity can do much to foster sound human relations. A teacher who leads children down paths of success in social studies, thereby making them feel good about themselves, may be nurturing some child's self-esteem for a lifetime.

Grade Level Examples

Kindergarten—Awareness of Self in a Social Setting

The major thrust of the kindergarten program should be to provide socialization experiences that help children bridge their home life with the group life of the school. Teachers can expect considerable variation in the extent of kindergartners' experience in group settings. Some have been in day-care centers or preschools for two or more years. Others are entering a social environment that involves several other children for the first time. Learning about the physical and social environments of the school will thus be different for individual children. Nevertheless, they all need to begin to learn the reasons for rules as required for orderly social relationships. Awareness of self should be developed through face-to-face relationships with others in social settings. It is important at this level to provide children with success experiences to help them develop self-esteem. Some structured experiences to sensitize children to a world of many and diverse peoples and cultures need to be included.

Grade 1—The Individual in Primary Social Groups: Understanding School and Family Life

The socialization to school begun in kindergarten should be continued and extended in 1st grade. Basic concepts related to social studies content should be introduced. Children can learn the specialized roles of school personnel as an example of division of labor. Family life and structure, including variations of family structures, should be included, as well as roles of family members. Essential activities of a family in meeting basic material and psychological needs should be stressed. Variations in the way families live need to be studied: e.g., urban, rural, self-employed, single-parent family arrangements, and various housing options. Dependence of family members on one another and of the family on other families should be stressed. Children should learn that the family is the primary support group for people everywhere. The need for rules and laws should be taught as a natural extension of orderly group life. History can be presented through the study of the children's own families and the study of family life in earlier times. Learning about family life in other cultures provides opportunities for comparing ways of living. The globe should be introduced along with simple maps to promote learning of geographic concepts and relationships. It is important that the program include some study of the world beyond the neighborhood. Direct experience and hands-on activities are essential at this level, but the program should be organized around specific social studies goals and objectives rather than consisting of unstructured play activities in social settings.

Grade 2—Meeting Basic Needs in Nearby Social Groups: The Neighborhood

Meeting basic requirements of living in nearby social groups should be the central theme in 2d grade. The program should emphasize that the neighborhood is the students' own unique place in space, and they should learn some of the ways their space interacts with the rest of the world. It is in the study of the neighborhood that students can and should learn on a firsthand basis some of the most elemental of human relationships such as sharing and caring, helping others in time of need, and living harmoniously with neighbors. The study of social functions such as education, production, consumption, communication, and transportation in a neighborhood context are appropriate as children develop an understanding and appreciation of people in groups. The need for rules and laws should be stressed and illustrated by examples from the everyday lives of children. Geographic concepts relating to direction and physical features of the landscape need to be included. A global perspective is important and can be sought through the study of neighborhood life in another culture. Contrasting neighborhood life today with what it was in an earlier time should also be included to provide historical perspective.

Grade 3—Sharing Earth Space with Others: The Community

The community in a global setting is the focus of study at the 3d grade level. The local community provides an excellent laboratory for the study of social life because all aspects of social living take place there. But the concept of community should not be limited to the local area. It is essential that some attention be given to the global community. Social functions such as production, transportation, communication, distribution, and government, including their international connections, should be stressed. The concepts of dependence and interdependence can be emphasized at the local, national, and international levels. Geographic concepts and skills should be extended to include the interactions of human beings with the environment. Place location and map-reading skills must be stressed. Some emphasis should be given to the study of the history of the local community, especially relevant social history and biographies of prominent local citizens.

Grade 4—Human Life in Varied Environments: The Region

The 4th grade is the ideal level to focus on basic geographic concepts and related skills. The major emphasis in the 4th grade is the region, an area of the earth that is defined for a specific reason. Where state regulations require it, the home state may be studied as a political region. World geographic regions defined in terms of physical features, climate, agricultural production, industrial development, or economic level should be selected for study. Culture regions of the past and present may also be included. There should be some variation in the regions selected for study to illustrate the adaptability of human beings to varied environments. All the basic map- and globe-reading skills should be included in the program. History should be included in the units of study to show how places have changed over time. Economic concepts such as *resources*, *scarcity*, and *exchange* should be used to illustrate how regions of the world interact.

Grade 5—People of the Americas: The United States and Its Close Neighbors

The 5th grade program focuses on the development of the United States as a nation in the Western Hemisphere, with particular emphasis on developing affective attachments to those principles on which this nation was founded and that guided its development. The diverse cultural, ethnic, and racial origins of the American people should be stressed. Attention should be directed to specific individuals who have contributed to the political, social, economic, and cultural life of the nation. The inclusion of biographies of prominent American men and women of diverse ethnic origins is essential to highlight values embraced by this society. The 5th grade program should familiarize learners with the history and geography of the closest neighbor nations of the United States: Canada and Mexico.

Grade 6—People and Cultures: Representative World Regions

The focus of the 6th grade program is on selected people and cultures of the Eastern Hemisphere and Latin America. The people and cultures should be representative of (1) major geographical regions of the world; (2) levels of economic development; (3) historical development; and (4) political and value systems. The interdependence of nations should be a major theme. Instruction needs to be directed toward understanding and appreciating the lifeways of other people through the development of such concepts as language, technology, institutions, and belief systems.

It is recommended that *at least* one semester of systematic study be devoted to Latin America in either the 6th *or* 7th grade. The cultural, political, and economic linkages with the United States should be emphasized. The growing importance of Latin America in international political and economic affairs should be stressed.

Grade 7—A Changing World of Many Nations: A Global View

The 7th grade program provides an opportunity to broaden the concept of humanity within a global context. The focus should be on the world as the home of many different people who strive to deal with the forces that shape their lives. The search for—and the need for—peaceful relations among nations needs to be stressed. The content is international in scope (including the Western Hemisphere), with a major emphasis on basic concepts from geography—resource distribution, spatial interaction, areal differentiation, global interdependence. The history of areas should be provided in order to illustrate changes through time. The aspirations and problems of developing nations need to be stressed. Emphasis should be given to the many interconnections that exist between places and people in the modern world. This not only includes resources necessary to support technologically based societies but cultural interconnections as well—arts, literature, communication, religion, music, and sports.

The 6th and 7th grade programs should emphasize geographic knowledge of the world and its people. Physical geography and place location should be stressed, along with such other geographic concepts as *spatial interaction, interdependence, resource development and use, international trade,* and *human habitation* with its effects on the environment. As was indicated in the 6th grade program, it is recommended that at least one semester of systematic study be devoted to Latin America in either the 6th or 7th grade.

Grade 8—Building a Strong and Free Nation: The United States

The 8th grade program is the study of the "epic of America," the development of the United States as a strong and free nation. The primary emphasis at this level should be the social history and economic development of the country, including cultural and aesthetic dimensions of the American experience. Attention should be given to the history of ordinary people doing ordinary things including family life, work, leisure, and medical care. The unique contribution of the men and women who built the heritage we share should be stressed. The presentation must be realistic and exciting to the early adolescent. This program should stress the important role played by the United States in global affairs and the need to secure peaceful relations with all nations.

(*Note:* Most students today complete high school and, therefore, take a full year of U.S. history in the 11th grade. Consequently, some school districts have adopted course options such as those listed on page 30 at the 8th grade level.)

Grade 9—Systems That Make a Democratic Society Work: Law, Justice, and Economics

The 9th grade program focuses on the concepts *social stability* and *social change* and calls for one semester of study of the law and justice systems and one semester of economics. A functional knowledge of the law and justice systems, as well as a knowledge of the economic system— along with related skills and attitudes—are critical to the practice of citizenship. These courses should address issues that capitalize on the real-life problems of students. They should also provide many opportunities for developing critical-thinking, problem-solving, and social-participation skills.

The 9th grade placement of this subject matter is critical in terms of the developmental needs of the early adolescent. Besides, some 9th graders will no longer be in school to take these courses as 12th graders. Problems of alienation and disengagement from law, justice, and economic systems are widespread among adolescents. Many are left with the feeling that they are powerless to cope with the forces that affect their lives. The integrated study of these systems, which make a democratic society work, *presented in ways that are perceived by young adolescents as meaningful to their lives,* should assist in helping young people develop a sense of needed efficacy in dealing with these systems.

(*Note:* In states where the study of state history and government is required by legislative mandate, basic concepts from law, justice, and economics can be incorporated in such a course.)

Grade 10—Origins of Major Cultures: A World History

The 10th grade program should focus on the history of the major cultures and societies of the contemporary world. The course stresses the diverse economic, political, religious, and social systems. Historical perspective should be provided on major world events and movements. Students should develop a knowledge of and an appreciation for the contributions of many cultures to the collective wisdom of the human race. The course should include attention to those historical differences among people that lead to conflict. The course is basically history and should help students learn the skills and tools of historical analysis. Nonetheless, it incorporates related concepts from other social science disciplines, especially anthropology, geography, political science, and economics.

Grade 11—The Maturing of America: United States History

The 11th grade program should be a comprehensive course in American history that is organized chronologically and serves as a capstone for the study of American history in the elementary and secondary schools. The forces that shaped and continue to shape political, economic, and social institutions should be studied. Changes in social and cultural values should also be included. The effects of growing international involvements and commitments must be stressed. The growth of the arts and literature, social reform movements, the extension of civil rights, the labor movement, and the growth of government should be included. The diversity of ethnic and racial origins of Americans and the effect of this diversity on the development of the nation should be emphasized.

Grade 12—One-year course or courses required; selection(s) to be made from the following:

Issues and Problems of Modern Society

Issues and problems of modern society should provide numerous opportunities for students to make a critical analysis of enduring social issues. The scope is broadened to emphasize the global dimensions of American problems and issues.

Introduction to the Social Sciences

The introduction to the social sciences should deal with the content and modes of inquiry of the social sciences.

The Arts in Human Societies

The arts in human societies should allow students to learn about the cultures of the world through the arts and literature.

International Area Studies

As an in-depth cross-cultural study of selected areas of the world, the course focuses on the interaction of different cultures in a defined area of the world.

Social Science Elective Courses

Anthropology, Economics, Government, Psychology, Sociology

Supervised Experience in Community Affairs

Local Options

It is not possible to present one scope and sequence that is appropriate for all the many communities that comprise such a large and diverse nation as the United States. Using this scope and sequence as a guide, school districts should have little difficulty modifying the grades K-5 curriculum to suit local needs and requirements. Grade 12 curriculum, however, may present problems for local curriculum developers; therefore, the Task Force is presenting three options in addition to the sequence developed on pages 25 to 29. All four options are summarized in chart 1.

Developing Democratic Beliefs and Values

Education to engender beliefs and values, including variations called moral education, attitude education, developing personal integrity, or character education, has been a persistent theme in American education from early colonial schools to the present. Long before the scientific study of society developed such concepts as group cohesiveness and shared values, people knew from their forebears' experience that individuals had to conduct themselves in ways consistent with a common set of beliefs and values if the behavior of individuals was to be predictable. Education in the home and in the school was designed to focus on those beliefs and values that translated into moral guidelines for citizens.

Chart 1. Optional Sequences for Grades 6-12

All the following options include:
1. One year of American history at grade 11
2. Systematic study of all major culture regions of the world
3. At least one semester of economics and one semester of law-related studies

Local school districts may develop a mix-and-match option to capitalize on local teacher strengths, availability of instructional materials, and community expectations. Such locally developed sequences should, however, include the three components listed in 1, 2, and 3 above.

	Grade 6	Grade 7	Grade 8	Grade 9	Grade 10	Grade 11	Grade 12
Option 1 See pages 22 to 29 for description of this option	People and Cultures: Representative world regions	A changing world of many nations: A global view	U.S. History with emphasis on social history and economic development	Economics and law-related studies (one semester each)	World history (both Western and non-Western)	U.S. history (chronological, political, social, economic)	Series of options: see page 29 for list of possibilities
Option 2	European cultures with their extension into the Western Hemisphere	A changing world of many nations: A global view	Economics and law-related studies (one semester each)	Cultures of the non-Western world	The Western heritage	U.S. History (chronological, political, social, economic)	Government (one semester); Issues and problems of modern society (one semester)
Option 3	Land and people of Latin America	People and cultures: Representative world regions	Interdisciplinary study of the local region (geographic, social, economic, historical) with an environmental emphasis	World history and cultures (2-year sequence)		U.S. History (chronological, political, social, economic)	Economics and law-related studies (one semester each)
Option 4	People and cultures: Representative world regions	A changing world of many nations: A global view	Interdisciplinary study of the local region (geographic, social, economic, historical) with an environmental emphasis	World cultures	The Western heritage	U.S. history (chronolgoical, political, social, economic)	Economics and law-related studies (one semester each)

Value consensus theory suggests that there is a set of core values in a society on which there is some measure of concurrence. These values are engendered in each succeeding generation, thereby making it possible for society to perpetuate itself beyond the life spans of individual citizens. As a matter of policy, the public clearly expects schools to inculcate those values on which there is consensus. State legislative mandates calling for the teaching of certain specific components of the social studies, such as state and national history, the Constitution, and economics, illustrate endorsements of certain beliefs and values associated with those subjects.

What democratic beliefs and values should be selected for the social studies program? "Essentials of Social Studies," a National Council for the Social Studies publication, lists *justice, equality, responsibility, freedom, diversity,* and *privacy* as essential. The NCSS "Social Studies Curriculum Guidelines" are based on the twin values of *rational process* and *human dignity*. One could add *rule of law, human rights, honesty,* and *equity* as other values that fall within the belief system of many Americans. But such lists of preferred democratic values must be anchored to valid sources if they are to be included in the school curriculum. For Americans, those sources are the basic social contracts of society—the Declaration of Independence, the Constitution of the United States, the Bill of Rights, and the legal and justice systems.

In the study of societies, students will be exposed to the ugly, the seamy, the hateful, and the violent. Although these qualities often characterize human behavior, there is also much in the human condition that is inspiring, uplifting, pleasing, and indeed beautiful. People *do* kill, maim, cheat, and torture one another, but they also produce paintings, music, literature, and perform charitable acts of great humaneness. Such contrasts and contradictions are typically human and can be found in various forms throughout the world. Young people should have the opportunity to see some of the beauty and decency that are part of the human potential.

Nothing can alter the reality that people live today in a changing, pluralistic society and are constantly confronted by clashes in values, controversy, and social change. Citizens need to be prepared to think, analyze, and support their views with reason and evidence. Society needs citizens who are capable of independent thinking and responsible social criticism. Society also needs citizens capable of thoughtful assessments of social situations through which they reach individual conclusions as they face unknown futures in which the traditional values they have been taught to cherish will be challenged and may require reevaluation.

The program of beliefs and values has to be based on something more than a collection of virtues that we would like to see in the "ideal" American. The main thrust of democratic beliefs and values is to guarantee the continuance of respect for human dignity and freedom. The following is a list of rights, freedoms, responsibilities, and beliefs that embody many of the common values embraced by Americans:

A. Rights of the Individual

   Right to life
   Right to liberty
   Right to dignity
   Right to security
   Right to equality of opportunity
   Right to justice
   Right to privacy
   Right to private ownership of property

B. Freedoms of the Individual

   Freedom to participate in the political process

Freedom of worship
Freedom of thought
Freedom of conscience
Freedom of assembly
Freedom of inquiry
Freedom of expression

C. **Responsibilities of the Individual**

To respect human life
To respect the rights of others
To be tolerant
To be honest
To be compassionate
To demonstrate self-control
To participate in the democratic process
To work for the common good
To respect the property of others

D. **Beliefs concerning Societal Conditions and Governmental Responsibilities**

Societies need laws that are accepted by the majority of the people.
Dissenting minorities are protected.
Government is elected by the people.
Government respects and protects individual rights.
Government respects and protects individual freedoms.
Government guarantees civil liberties.
Government works for the common good.

How and when should democratic beliefs and values be taught in the K-12 social studies curriculum? Both direct and indirect methods of teaching values are appropriate under certain conditions. Direct methods include the identification and examination of the value dimension of social issues, the selection of specific values for intensive study and analysis, resolution of value conflicts, and exploring consequences of decisions based on particular values. When using direct methods of teaching values, teachers should be aware that knowing about values does not mean that students have internalized them. That is, they may deal with values intellectually but not accept them as standards to guide their behavior.

Indirect methods have to do with the context within which values are taught and learned. The school and classroom environments, the example set by the teachers and other school authorities, are powerful forces in teaching and learning beliefs and values. The instructional environment should mirror the beliefs and values promoted in the social studies curriculum. When this happens, even 1st graders can learn through experience something about the meaning of justice, even though it will be years before they deal with justice as an abstract concept. Conversely, it is more difficult for high school teachers to teach the value of citizen participation in decision making when students see no evidence of their own involvement in decision making in their school. Teachers should recognize and take advantage of the many opportunities to teach democratic beliefs and values that present themselves in ordinary daily life at school and to provide experiences in which students can be personally involved. This means an unqualified respect for reason and diversity, a commitment to democratic values, an openness to alternative points of view, and a balanced treatment of issues on which competent persons have honest differences.

Related democratic beliefs and values are an important part of all subject matter included in the social studies. All social studies teachers at every grade level share responsibility for teaching them. Chart 2 provides illustrations of ways to include various democratic beliefs and values in the program of each grade level. Some of the illustrations reflect life conditions

Grade	Central Focus	Democratic Rights, Freedoms, Responsibilities, or Beliefs Addressed	Illustrations of Opportunities
K	Awareness of self in a social setting	1. Right to security 2. Right to equal opportunity 3. Respect for others' rights 4. Honesty	1. Explore how rules make a room safe for everyone. 2. Every child is scheduled to be a leader for a day. 3. Focus on common courtesies; e.g., when someone speaks, one should listen. 4. The teacher reinforces honesty as exhibited by children.
1	The individual in primary social groups	1. Impartiality 2. Freedom of worship 3. Consideration for others	1. When an altercation is reported, the teacher tries to find out exactly what happened before taking action. 2. Stress that each family decides whether or not or how to worship. 3. Everyone has a right to a turn.
2	Meeting basic needs in nearby social groups	1. Respect for property 2. Respect for laws 3. Value personal integrity	1. Discuss vandalism in neighborhoods. 2. Laws protect the safety of people. 3. Explore the importance of keeping promises.
3	Sharing Earth space with others	1. Pursuing individual and group goals 2. Government works for the common good	1. Goods are exchanged with other places to meet the needs of the people. 2. Government is concerned about the unemployed and works to reduce unemployment.
4	Human life in varied environments	1. Respect for the rights of others 2. Respect for different ways of living	1. Respect the right of individuals from other cultures to have different values. 2. Appreciate that life-styles of people in other places are different from ours.
5	People of the Americas	1. Freedom to worship 2. Right of privacy 3. Freedom of assembly	1. People came to the Americas because of religious persecution. 2. A home cannot be searched without a warrant except under most unusual circumstances. 3. Laws may not prohibit people from getting together in groups for any lawful purpose.
6	People and cultures	1. Governments respect and protect individual freedoms 2. Right to life 3. Right to justice	1. Compare the record of various governments in protecting individual freedoms. 2. Study societies in which individual human rights are not respected. 3. Examine various types of judicial systems.
7	A changing world of many nations	1. Freedom to participate in the political process 2. Right to equality of opportunity 3. Use of government to guarantee civil liberties	1. Discuss the anticolonial movement in parts of the world. 2. Discuss social class systems in various parts of the world. 3. Debate the status of civil liberties in developing nations.
8	Building a strong and free nation	1. Right to liberty 2. Participation in the democratic process 3. Freedom of expression	1. Discuss the injustices of slavery. 2. Analyze the voting record of Americans and particularly that of young people. 3. Study the debates and compromises reached in the development of the Constitution.
9	Systems that make a democratic society work	1. Right to equal opportunity 2. The common good 3. Compassion and sympathy	1. Study the opportunities people have to earn a living in various societies. 2. Debate the extent to which economic systems favor the common good. 3. Learn how effectively systems demonstrate compassion and sympathy for the poor and destitute.
10	Origins of major cultures	1. Freedom of thought 2. Societies' need for laws 3. Right to justice	1. Discuss the free-thinking spirit of the people of Ancient Greece. 2. Discuss the early Roman legal system. 3. Discuss the justice system in the various great civilizations of the past.
11	The maturing of America (U.S. history)	1. Right to life 2. Right to liberty 3. Right to justice	1. Debate the issues surrounding capital punishment. 2. Debate the issue of big government vs. the rights of the individual. 3. Discuss the role of medical, judicial, social, and psychological expertise in securing justice for victims of crimes as well as offenders.
12	Citizenship in a modern society: facing issues and problems	1. The common good 2. Right to security 3. Right to justice	1. Analyze whether or not problems are solved through the rational process or on the basis of vested interests. 2. Discuss value conflicts surrounding national security: Should we rely on more guns or on more and better education? 3. Discuss why proportionately more minority than majority offenders are convicted by the courts.

Chart 2. Illustrative Examples of Applications of Democratic Beliefs and Values

in school; others relate to the subject matter studied. *These are examples only and should not be construed as a recommended curriculum.*

Research finds that youth who are most supportive of democratic principles are those who practice investigation of issues in an open, supportive environment in the classroom. Therefore, by encouraging inquiry into social issues, social studies teachers build support for democratic values at the same time they develop skills needed by citizens in their local, national, and global communities. In studying the illustrative examples of applications of democratic values and beliefs above, teachers can identify issues for inquiry and decision making that are related to the subject matter studied that year and that are appropriate to the level of maturity of the children in the class.

Skills in the Social Studies Curriculum

To have a *skill* means that one is able to do something proficiently in repeated performances. Such things are done automatically, almost without thinking about them. Reading, knowing how to find a book in the library, participating in a group discussion, and finding a place on a map are examples of a few skills important to the social studies. They are critical to achievement, because without them students cannot meet the requirements and expectations of the social studies program. Skills, then, are important vehicles in learning concepts, searching for information, gaining insight into values and beliefs, and in learning other skills.

Learning skills requires sequential development, systematic instruction, and practice. Using and applying skills are the best forms of practice, and most social studies skills should be taught in functional settings. In an appropriate instructional sequence, simple variants of the skill are introduced at early levels, with more sophisticated applications in the upper grades. The sequence in which skills are introduced, developed, and reinforced should be determined by conditions unique to particular school populations and, therefore, must be developed at the local level.

The Task Force has searched the literature and has selected those skills that are most relevant to the social studies and presents them in chart 3 following a problem-solving sequence. The list begins with skills in acquiring information, moves to skills in organizing and using information, and progresses to skills needed for effective social participation. Each of these categories of skills should appear in some form in the curriculum of every grade, K-12. The list can be used by teachers, curriculum developers, and local education agencies and committees as a guide in developing their own programs.

Regional Task Force Members: Chair: *John Jarolimek, Professor Emeritus, College of Education, University of Washington, Seattle; *Susan Austin, Senior Research Associate, Research for Better Schools, Philadelphia, Pennsylvania; Franklin D. Carlson, Professor, Central Washington University, Ellensburg; Catherine K. Henderson, Elementary School Teacher, Highline School District, Seattle, Washington; Allen Johnston, Jr., High School Teacher and District Social Studies Coordinator, Shoreline School District, Seattle, Washington; *Theodore Kaltsounis, Professor of Education, College of Education, University of Washington, Seattle; Kenneth E. Leonard, Office of University Advancement, Seattle Pacific University, Seattle, Washington; *Elizabeth O. Pearson, Senior High School Teacher, Renton, Washington; *Jack Rogers, Elementary School Teacher, Shoreline School District, Seattle, Washington; *Larry Strickland, Washington State Social Studies Supervisor, Olympia.*

*Members whose names are marked with an asterisk contributed to the 1989 revision of the Task Force Report.

Notes

1. The Task Force acknowledges the thoughtful and substantial contribution of several committees that have produced officially sanctioned curriculum documents for the National Council for the Social Studies. These publications extend as far back as the mid-1950s and include "A Guide to Content in the Social Studies" (1957), "The Social Studies and the National Interest" (1962), "Social Studies in Transition: Guidelines for Change" (1965), "Social Studies Curriculum Guidelines" (1971, revised in 1979), "Curriculum Guidelines for Multiethnic Education" (1976), "Essentials of the Social Studies" (1981), and "Social Studies for Early Childhood and Elementary School Children Preparing for the 21st Century" (1988).
2. Much of the material in this section reflects the views expressed in the NCSS statement, "Essentials of the Social Studies," approved by the Board of Directors of the council in 1981, and the NCSS "Social Studies Curriculum Guidelines," 1971, 1979.

Chart 3. Essential Skills for Social Studies

Suggested strength of instructional effort:
- ▬ Minimum or none
- ▬▬ Some
- ▬▬▬ Major
- ■ Intense

I. Skills Related to Acquiring Information

A. Reading Skills

1. Comprehension

K-3 4-6 7-9 10-12

- Read to get literal meaning
- Use chapter and section headings, topic sentences, and summary sentences to select main ideas
- Differentiate main and subordinate ideas
- Select passages that are pertinent to the topic studied
- Interpret what is read by drawing inferences
- Detect cause and effect relationships
- Distinguish between fact and opinion; recognize propaganda
- Recognize author bias
- Use picture clues and picture captions to aid comprehension
- Use literature to enrich meaning
- Read for a variety of purposes: critically, analytically, to predict outcomes, to answer a question, to form an opinion, to skim for facts
- Read various forms of printed material: books, magazines, newspapers, directories, schedules, journals

2. Vocabulary

- Use usual word attach skills: sight recognition, phonetic analysis, structural analysis
- Use context clues to gain meaning
- Use appropriate sources to gain meaning of essential terms and vocabulary: glossary, dictionary, text, word lists
- Recognize and understand an increasing number of social studies terms

3. Rate of Reading

- Adjust speed of reading to suit purpose
- Adjust rate of reading to difficulty of the material

B. Study Skills

1. Find Information

- Use various parts of a book (index, table of contents, etc.)
- Use key words, letters on volumes, index, and cross references to find information
- Evaluate sources of information—print, visual, electronic
- Use the community as a resource

2. Arrange Information in Usable Forms

- Make outline of topic
- Prepare summaries
- Make timelines
- Take notes
- Keep records
- Use italics, marginal notes, and footnotes
- Listen for information
- Follow directions
- Write reports and research papers
- Prepare a bibliography

C. Reference and Information-Search Skills

1. The Library

- Use card catalog to locate books
- Use *Readers' Guide to Periodical Literature* and other indexes
- Use COMCATS (Computer Catalog Service)
- Use public library telephone information service

2. Special References

- Almanacs
- Encyclopedias
- Dictionary
- Indexes
- Government publications
- Microfiche
- Periodicals
- News sources: newspapers, news magazines, TV, radio, videotapes, artifacts

3. Maps, Globes, Graphics

Use map- and globe-reading skills:
- Orient a map and note directions
- Locate places on map and globe
- Use scale and compute distances
- Interpret map symbols and visualize what they mean
- Compare maps and make inferences
- Express relative location
- Interpret graphs
- Detect bias in visual material
- Interpret social and political messages of cartoons
- Interpret history through artifacts

4. Community Resources

- Use sources of information in the community
- Conduct interviews of individuals in the community
- Use community newspapers

D. Technical Skills Unique to Electronic Devices

1. Computer

- Operate a computer using prepared instructional or reference programs
- Operate a computer to enter and retrieve information gathered from a variety of sources

2. Telephone and Television Information Networks

- Ability to access information through networks

II. Skills Related to Organizing and Using Information

A. Thinking Skills

1. Classify Information
   - Identify relevant factual material
   - Sense relationship between items of factual information
   - Group data in categories according to appropriate criteria
   - Place in proper sequence:
     (1) order of occurrence
     (2) order of importance
   - Place data in tabular form: charts, graphs, illustrations

2. Interpret Information
   - State relationships between categories of information
   - Note cause and effect relationships
   - Draw inferences from factual material
   - Predict likely outcomes based on factual information
   - Recognize the value dimension of interpreting factual material
   - Recognize instances in which more than one interpretation of factual material is valid

3. Analyze Information
   - Form a simple organization of key ideas related to a topic
   - Separate a topic into major components according to appropriate criteria
   - Examine critically relationships between and among elements of a topic
   - Detect bias in data presented in various forms: graphics, tabular, visual, print
   - Compare and contrast credibility of differing accounts of the same event

4. Summarize Information
   - Extract significant ideas from supporting, illustrative details
   - Combine critical concepts into a statement of conclusions based on information
   - Restate major ideas of a complex topic in concise form
   - Form opinion based on critical examination of relevant information
   - State hypotheses for further study

5. Synthesize Information
   - Propose a new plan of operation, create a new system, or devise a futuristic scheme based on available information
   - Reinterpret events in terms of what *might* have happened, and show the likely effects on subsequent events
   - Present visually (chart, graph, diagram, model, etc.) information extracted from print
   - Prepare a research paper that requires a creative solution to a problem
   - Communicate orally and in writing

6. Evaluate Information
   - Determine whether or not the information is pertinent to the topic
   - Estimate the adequacy of the information
   - Test the validity of the information, using such criteria as source, objectivity, technical correctness, currency

B. Decision-Making Skills
   - Identify a situation in which a decision is required
   - Secure needed factual information relevant to making the decision
   - Recognize the values implicit in the situation and the issues that flow from them
   - Identify alternative courses of action and predict likely consequences of each
   - Make decision based on the data obtained
   - Take action to implement the decision

C. Metacognitive Skills
   - Select an appropriate strategy to solve a problem
   - Self-monitor one's thinking process

III. Skills Related to Interpersonal Relationships and Social Participation

A. Personal Skills
   - Express personal convictions
   - Communicate own beliefs, feelings, and convictions
   - Adjust own behavior to fit the dynamics of various groups and situations
   - Recognize the mutual relationship between human beings in satisfying one another's needs

B. Group Interaction Skills
   - Contribute to the development of a supportive climate in groups
   - Participate in making rules and guidelines for group life
   - Serve as a leader or follower
   - Assist in setting goals for the group
   - Participate in delegating duties, organizing, planning, making decisions, and taking action in a group setting
   - Participate in persuading, compromising, debating, and negotiating in the resolution of conflicts and differences

C. Social and Political Participation Skills
   - Keep informed on issues that affect society
   - Identify situation in which social action is required
   - Work individually or with others to decide on an appropriate course of action
   - Work to influence those in positions of social power to strive for extensions of freedom, social justice, and human rights
   - Accept and fulfill social responsibilities associated with citizenship in a free society

Social Studies Themes and Questions to Reflect Principles and Practices in a Democracy

H. Michael Hartoonian and Margaret A. Laughlin

> *Chivalry, the dominant political idea of the ruling class, left as great a gap between ideal and practice as religion. The ideal was a vision of order maintained by the warrior class and formulated in the image of the Round Table, nature's perfect shape. King Arthur's knights adventured for the right against dragons, enchanters, and wicked men, establishing order in a wild world. So their living counterparts were supported, in theory, to serve as defenders of the Faith, upholders of justice, champions of the oppressed. In practice, they were themselves the oppressors, and by the 14th Century the violence and lawlessness of men of the sword had become a major agency of disorder. When the gap between ideal and real becomes too wide, the system breaks down. Legend and story have always reflected this.*
>
> —Barbara W. Tuchman

Is the gap between ideals and practice too wide today? How can we establish greater congruency between our social, ethical, and educational theories and what we do in our schools?

Although Barbara Tuchman (1978) articulates a situation in 14th-century Europe, the parallels to our contemporary world should not be overlooked by the reader. The important general idea for us, however, is the discrepancy between principle and practice. From our vantage point today, educators must see the relevancy of this dynamic to social studies curriculum and instruction. Do classroom practices reflect educational principles?

Curriculum Design as Dialogue

The design for curriculum development suggested here is based upon the assumption that specific scope and sequence decisions should be made by local curriculum committees and teachers. For the most part, these decisions are political. They are decisions based upon the authority and power of individuals and groups and are steeped in tradition and the conventional wisdom of the profession—aided, we hope, by research.

It is our intention to suggest an approach to curriculum decision making based upon a series of necessary (though not sufficient) themes and questions that can initiate a dialogue about the logical, philosophical, and psychological relevance of scope and sequence (ideals) to the teaching, learning, and context of social studies instruction (practice).

Rationale

Education must always be defined within the context of a particular society. This is the case primarily because education is responsible for maintaining and passing on the cultural heritage (ideals) and improving self and society (real). This requires freedom and continual criticism, including the opportunity to search for truth and to test ideas. Basic to ongoing criticism is the availability of information from numerous sources, the continual refining of communication skills, development of intellectual abilities, and respect for self and others.

Improvement of civilization incorporates the thoughtful consideration of change (history), an understanding of the workings of society (social sciences), and the courage to act upon reasoned convictions (ethical policy-making). Schools have a major responsibility in determining the quality of civilization by providing new generations with knowledge, abilities, attitudes, and perspectives that permit freedom, continual criticism of, and improvement in our quality of life.

Certainly, other social institutions such as the family, church, and media also have responsibilities to transmit information and knowledge important to the development of informed and thoughtful citizens. In a democratic republic, however, education becomes even more important because our system is built upon the concept of the "enlightened citizen"—that is, an individual in touch with the cultural heritage; an individual possessing a working knowledge of the economic, political, and social forces that make up the human ecosystem in which we all must function; an individual who understands the principles of the rule of law, legal limits to freedom, and majority rule with minority rights; and an individual who possesses the attitude of fair play, seeks cooperation, and demands quality in the character and work of self and others. Without a conscious effort to teach and learn these things, a free republic will not long endure. Thus our first priority—our first public-policy goal—is to ensure our survival as a free nation through the development of enlightened citizens.

Social studies education is fundamental to the primary purpose of schooling. It constitutes the school subjects most directly concerned with the study of civilization, the development of reflective thinking, and the improvement of society through enlightened civic and social participation. Although this responsibility falls partly on other segments of the curriculum, it is the social studies that assume direct responsibility for students to study and practice making personal and public-policy decisions as a part of their ongoing citizenship responsibilities. The following scope and sequence design presents and represents a way of thinking about the social studies curriculum consistent with these responsibilities.

Goals

Social studies content is concerned with developing reflective, democratic citizenship within a global context and includes the disciplines typically classified as belonging to the social and behavioral sciences as well as history, geography, and content selected from law, philosophy, humanities, and mathematics. It also includes those topics and issues that focus on social problems, issues, and controversies. The social studies can be oriented to one discipline or multiple disciplines, depending upon the topic selected for study. Social studies programs address four educational goals:

- The development of enlightened democratic citizenship for effective participation in local, state, national, and international affairs
- The appreciation and understanding of our cultural heritage, including diversity and its role in contemporary society
- The acquisition of academic knowledge and abilities related to the study of the motives, actions, and consequences of human beings as they live individually as well as in groups and societies in a variety of place and time settings; and the joy of learning about self, others, and human history
- Learning "how to learn"—how to use prior knowledge to understand complex ideas and how to create new ideas

All these goals are of equal importance, for they reinforce each other. Thus the goal of citizenship is supported by the goals of discipline, academic study, and ongoing learning. Stated another way, the student should be able to:

- Use reasoning processes in economic, political, social, and personal policy-making
- Appreciate and value the diversity and commonality of the human family throughout history

- Comprehend the vocabulary, logic, and methodology of the several academic disciplines that make up the social studies
- Communicate ideas through speaking, listening, writing, and other use of symbols
- Use the social and natural sciences, history, geography, literature, social mathematics (statistics, probability, social indicators, data-based management systems), and the fine arts to describe and explain social phenomena
- Understand the importance of values in the lives of people and how values influence our behavior both as individuals and as a society

Most important, a thorough understanding of the social studies can provide for the development of perspective. Perspective is understanding or wisdom gained by a temporal and spatial knowledge that transcends the present setting and enables one to ask such important questions as, What is the good society? What is the good person? What obligations do I have to the ideals and people of the past, present, and future? What is the proper relationship between the individual and the state? How and to what extent should I be involved with people and institutions on this globe? To what extent is our civilization likely to endure? What values do we wish to preserve? What heritage should we leave for future generations?

Program Scope: Major Curriculum Themes

The particular curriculum design suggested here is based upon ten themes that extend logically from the previously identified goals. These themes are included at each grade level with increasing sophistication and constitute, in large measure, the program scope. The themes help define the program's scope to the extent that they present perspectives that provide students the temporal, spatial, and cultural criteria necessary for comprehension and rational action. To some degree, any delineation of major themes is arbitrary. Whereas different themes may be emphasized at various grade levels, they should be included at every grade and may be presented in any coherent order based on the maturity level and ability of the students.

With the above in mind, examine figure 1.

Scope
Grade Levels
K 1 2 3 4 5 6 7 8 9 10 11 12

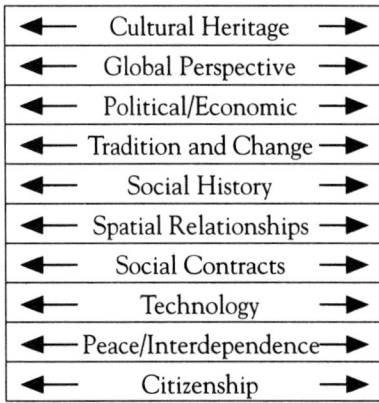

Fig. 1. Major scope and curriculum themes

Cultural Heritage

The cultural heritage of a people is embodied in stories about their values, hopes and dreams, and fears and dilemmas. The major responsibility of the school is to transmit the cultural heritage to the next generation. This is accomplished by putting students in touch with history—the people, ideals, artifacts, and dilemmas of the past that need to be brought forward as a part of our present and future.

Every human society (and group within larger modern societies) has particular patterns of behavior that make up its culture. A culture consists of language, tools, important documents, customs, social institutions, beliefs, rituals, games, attitudes, utensils, clothing, ornaments, works of art, religion, and more. Within social groups, individuals learn accepted means of meeting their needs and coping with problems of living in groups. These ways of perceiving, thinking, and behaving are part of their heritage.

Global Perspective

Notions of "global community," "spaceship earth," "the shrinking globe," and "global interdependence" abound in popular literature. Every society struggles with the ongoing conflict between the desire for independence and the realities of interdependence. The world is becoming more crowded, more interconnected, and more volatile. There is the desire for peace but the preparation for war continues. What happens in the most distant part of the world may quickly affect us.

Students need to understand the distinctions between political and cultural maps. This distinction suggests that culture is not necessarily confined to political boundaries. Students must also understand the worldwide dynamic of the human, technological, and ideological distance as culture is shared across the world. Interdependence demands that our perspective be global.

Political/Economic

One of the fundamental attributes of a citizen of the Republic is the ability to function effectively within its political and economic systems. This means the ability to make personal and social decisions and judge the decisions of others often with little time and incomplete information. From serving on local political-action groups to understanding monetary and fiscal policy, students need experience in the disciplined study of economics and political science. Citizens need to become aware of their political and economic opportunities and obligations.

To a large extent, citizens still see their civic roles as public and their economic roles as private. We see all "civic" citizens as equal because of the one person/one vote concept, but we see "economic" citizens as unequal because of their different standards of living. Within the Republic, the citizen must understand the relationships between civic and economic justice and power and work for the public good as well as the private good.

Tradition and Change

People, events, tools, institutions, attitudes, values, and ideas all change over time. History records the struggles of people and groups who favor change and those who oppose change. The rate of change is uneven among and within different cultures and societies, but change is continuous and the rate of change in today's world is accelerating.

As the rate of change accelerates, we must place greater importance than in the past on anticipating the future. Clearly, we cannot accurately predict the future, but we can envision various scenarios and be ready for more than one possibility. Futurists have developed a useful kit of processes for dealing with the future. These include cross-impact matrix, scenario writing, trend extrapolation, brainstorming, and technological assessment.

Important as change is in our lives, we must recognize that human experience is continuous and interrelated. Continuity and traditions are facts of life and provide life with meaning, beauty, and truth. In some ways, "nothing new occurs under the sun." All persons, events, actions, and change are the outcome of things that have gone before. We are inevitably products of our past and in some ways restricted by it. Students should learn how change and continuity constantly influence their lives.

Social History

The need for equity, justice, and a large reservoir of historical and contemporary evidence demands that we include women, minorities, and the so-called ordinary people in our study of the human family. Human values come to life through the stories of people who played many roles in the drama of history. For example, children can learn about courage from stories and teachers can use the songs and poetry of the downtrodden to teach about justice.

Ideas about work, sorrow, and joy are to be found in letters and journals of many who are not "real" authors or authorities. Social history encourages the study of the past—through primary sources and personal accounts. When concerned with the study or process of history—doing history—the student will discover the texture and grace reported in those narratives that somehow have not found their way into full view in textbooks and other materials.

Spatial Relationships

The study of area distribution, the examination of particular places, and the delineation of regions helps students understand how earth space is organized. People use similar earth space or areas in different ways. They line or interconnect the different areas with transportation and communication routes. They move themselves, messages, and goods and services over the routes. They conduct their government and engage in various types of activities, such as religious or recreational, within particular spatial arrangements.

The discipline most involved with spatial relationships is geography. Geography is concerned with understanding the location and spatial arrangements of places and landscapes on the earth. Simply knowing the location or the spatial distribution, however, is not enough. Students also need to learn the causes and consequences of such spatial arrangements.

As part of their study, students need to develop a knowledge of the physical earth itself—its size, shape, movements, and the materials and natural processes of its surface. They should learn to build mental-image maps of the spatial arrangements over the earth of different kinds of phenomena. This skill begins early and the mental maps increase in number and refinement with each year of maturity.

The study of geography not only includes people and almost all their activities, but also the earth and earth processes. Consequently, geography links the social and the natural sciences and provides the spatial perspective necessary in understanding culture and human behavior.

Social Contracts

The idea that one is part of a society also affirms that we enter into a social contract with our fellow citizens. This contract outlines our public behavior and defines our privileges and obligations as citizens. In a sense, this contract provides the criteria for our ethical behavior from civility to jurisprudence. One must come to respect the full citizenship of those who are different, those who have different backgrounds and talents, and those who take unpopular positions on social issues.

Social contracts are entered into not only by people as they approach the age of majority, they are also a real and necessary part of the society we call family, school, athletics, social clubs, and other social organizations. The social contract suggests that we are social and political at the same time, and it is crucial that within the democratic republic citizens understand not only the contours of the contract but the fine print as well.

Technology

Technology and science constitute an inclusive set. That is, the line between these notions is unclear. As humans modify nature for their purposes they engage in both science and engineering. Technology can also be understood as one of our "tools." We use these tools in utilitarian as well as aesthetic ways to bring comfort, meaning, enjoyment, and danger to our lives.

We also see and understand the world through tools that cause us to think in certain ways. Tools are thoughts as much as thoughts are tools. In many ways we are extensions of our tools. We see, hear, travel, fight, and stay alive because of tools (technology). Given the facts of the Information Age, data and technologies are so pervasive in our lives and the lives of most of the world's people that we, indeed, do see and understand the natural and social worlds only within the frameworks of the tools we use. Social studies education must help students understand the role of technology in their lives.

Peace/Interdependence

Today, one hears cries for peace in many languages and from many nations. Is peace the absence of war and violence? Is peace the same as law and order? Are there forms of violence, such as child abuse, spouse abuse, physical and psychological torture, imprisonment without trial, or starvation, that occur under seemingly peaceful conditions? Human rights are violated to some degree in most countries of the world. In those nations where conditions are the worst, people may react violently to resist the violence of their system. How can an understanding of the need for justice be incorporated into the plea for peace? The tree of peace has its roots in justice. If there are no roots, the tree dies. The two concepts of *peace* and *justice* are inseparable.

Great differences of opinion exist on how best to attain peace. Some advocate peace through military strength. Others prefer reliance on removing the causes of conflict. Human knowledge of military strength far surpasses knowledge of conflict resolution. The latter is largely in the realm of social sciences and deserves attention—even by those who wish to retain armed strength as a last resort. Our sophistication in avoiding armed conflict must be upgraded to match our proficiency in conducting military actions.

Every society struggles with the conflict between the desire for independence and the realities of interdependence. Modern economic systems are based on the principle of specialization because it is more efficient and productive than other ways of getting work done. Specialization occurs when we produce a narrower range of goods or services than we consume. Individuals, businesses, regions, or nations, can practice specialization. Specialization therefore has a spatial as well as an economic component. Specialization results from the division of labor, where productive tasks are divided among workers to take advantage of a worker's skill at a specific production operation.

When an economic society is based on specialization, as most modern economies are, economic interdependence is an inevitable consequence. A breakdown of a single part of an interdependent production system can seriously disrupt output, even stopping production completely. Every student should understand that the benefits gained from specialization come at the cost of increased vulnerability to disruption of an interdependent system. Interdependence suggests that our perspective must be global and subject to revision as new actions and inventions shape our world.

Citizenship

Citizenship in a democracy involves both obligations and privileges. Students need to understand how government and politics actually work. They need to understand the underlying purposes and values of government in a free society. In social studies classes students should have opportunities to develop the abilities required to be effective citizens in a democratic society. Students need opportunities to learn and practice their roles, rights, and responsibilities as citizens of a democracy and members of the global community.

To help students become effective citizens in a democratic society, social studies classes should be designed to develop informed and analytical policymakers who are committed and involved in their community. The notion of citizenship extends to serving the community through volunteer work, participating in policy-action groups, writing letters to the editor, voting, and being able to express coherent ideas and opinions about civic issues.

In organizing the social studies curriculum, appropriate attention needs to be given to study of values. Students also need to have opportunities to reflect on their values and those of society.

Social Studies and Higher-Order Thinking

Social studies content and higher-order thinking are seen here in two different but *interrelated* ways. First, social studies content is viewed as a story about continuity and change over time—an exciting narrative or analytical study about people, events, and issues (Danto 1965). Second, social studies may be understood as a disciplined study or inquiry involving the creation, structuring, and use of knowledge (Bragaw and Hartoonian 1988). Thinking within the social studies curriculum should address both these ideas. Thus, social studies may be both an artful narrative *and* a set of assumptions, concepts, explanations, and biases that reflect the attitudes and craft of the community of scholars, including students and teachers, who construct social knowledge. A closer look at thinking in the social studies disciplines (history, geography, the social and behavioral sciences, and, in some cases, the humanities) reveals the use of concepts such as narrative, change, continuity, chronology, cause and effect relationships, evidence, and frame of reference. In other words, history and the social sciences can be defined as recorded narratives or stories about the past or present that describe change and continuity over time and seek to explain change and continuity through a series of cause and effect propositions based on evidence and shaped by the scholar's social frame of reference. We all attempt to find out not only what happened but why it happened, what trends can be suggested, and how and why humans behave in certain ways in different social settings. Some of the most important questions we consider when thinking about the past, present, and future of the social world include:

- How can we best conceptualize a topic, issue, theme, event, or behavior?
- What defines a historical period? What defines a theme? What defines an issue?
- What constitutes primary and secondary evidence? How can such evidence be evaluated and used? What evidence is missing?
- How are cause and effect relationships handled in a narrative or discourse?

The dynamic use of these questions and the concepts they embrace are fundamental to the way in which we conduct social inquiry. That is, the way in which we think about and with social knowledge is directly related to the concepts and questions we use and their relationship to one another. In social studies, as in most other fields of inquiry, there are several basic interrelated components of critical study involved in the construction and use of knowledge. They constitute the necessary elements in thinking about personal and social questions, and present a model for higher-order or reflective thinking. These components are identified here as (1) comprehension or conceptualization, (2) causality, (3) validity of explanation, and (4) creative extension. Let us look at these components one at a time.

The first or most fundamental level of study is for students to *conceptualize* the people, setting, story, or context of the phenomenon they are studying. At this level, the following questions are asked: What is going on? How have things changed? And, how have they remained the same? These kinds of questions help define the temporal and spatial context necessary for comprehending the issue, problem, topic, or theme studied. *Comprehension* also includes the knowledge and skills that students bring to the inquiry. What factual knowledge of major social or historical movements and cultures and what knowledge of the content and methods of the social science disciplines do the students have? As part of the process of comprehension, students must understand data in textual, visual, and quantitative form so as to be able to relate new contexts to previously learned data and knowledge, and to identify problems or issues.

The second level of study deals with *causality*. Once students conceptualize and comprehend the setting of the inquiry, they must then ask how and why the setting acquired its characteristics. Their inquiry should allow them to formulate cause and effect relationships and use logic in their own explanations of social and historical developments and to look for logic in the explanations of others. Specifically, students must use skills of analysis to help them gain some understanding of how to approach the problem of change over time and to recognize and explain major events, trends, or issues.

At the third level, students inquire into the accuracy or *validity* of the explanations suggested previously. Here students investigate bias, the nature of evidence, and the methods of evaluation used to validate explanations. To do this, students must have some familiarity with the techniques of quantitative and nonquantitative analysis as well as the ability to deal with diverse interpretations of data and to think critically about conflicting interpretations.

Finally, the fourth level of study is concerned with *creative extensions*; that is, students' creative inquiry into new settings and issues. Creativity and independent study abilities and skills are paramount at this level as students seek to combine insight and experience with logic to gain new knowledge. Here students begin to develop their own interpretations by establishing linkages and seeing connections between different historical or contemporary events and probing issues of causation and outcome. They also expand their use of knowledge by linking the past with the present and exploring the historical developments underlying present similarities and differences among the world's peoples. In sum, this fourth level interrelates with all other levels, thus creating the dynamics of what we understand as the conduct of inquiry and the nature of critical discourse.

Once again, it should be noted that neither the four components of study (comprehension and conceptualization, causality, validity of explanation, and creative extension) nor their related skills and abilities are mutually exclusive. The components do, however, suggest activities in which students should be engaged if they are to understand social inquiry. These activities are crucial for equipping students with the ability to communicate (listen, speak, discuss, and write) not only about interesting historical and contemporary social issues but also about the quality and accuracy of social inquiry itself. These skills with varying degrees of sophistication can be used throughout the social studies curriculum.

The Context of Instruction and Social Inquiry

Operationally and as an example, let us look at the relationship between reasoning or higher-order thinking and content within the environment (setting) of a high school history class. Although the following example addresses the teaching of history, it has application in any social studies class. What is critical to all aspects of study and thinking is the ability to comprehend or conceptualize, to deal with causality, to explore validity or truth claims, and to create extensions to new settings or disciplines within a learning environment that nurtures inquiry. John Dewey suggested (1916, 18-22) that the development of the attitudes and dispositions necessary to the continuous and progressive life of a society cannot take place by direct conveyance of belief, emotions, and knowledge. It takes place, he thought, through the intermediary of the environment. The environment consists of the sum total of conditions that are concerned in the execution of the activity characteristics of a living being.

Let us consider a lesson about the Great Depression of the 1930s. This might be a lesson within a U.S. history course at the 10th or 11th grade. One of the first things that usually occurs in such a course is that level-one *conceptualization/comprehension* teaching takes place. That is, the teacher wants students to know the setting, story, and context of the topic under study. What is going on here? How is this different from or similar to previously studied periods? In other words, the instructor wants students to conceptualize the theme, topic, or concept in terms of time, place, and circumstance. From this point, teacher and students move to the second level of inquiry.

At level two, consideration is given to *causality*. How can we explain why the depression occurred? What were the causes and consequences of the depression?

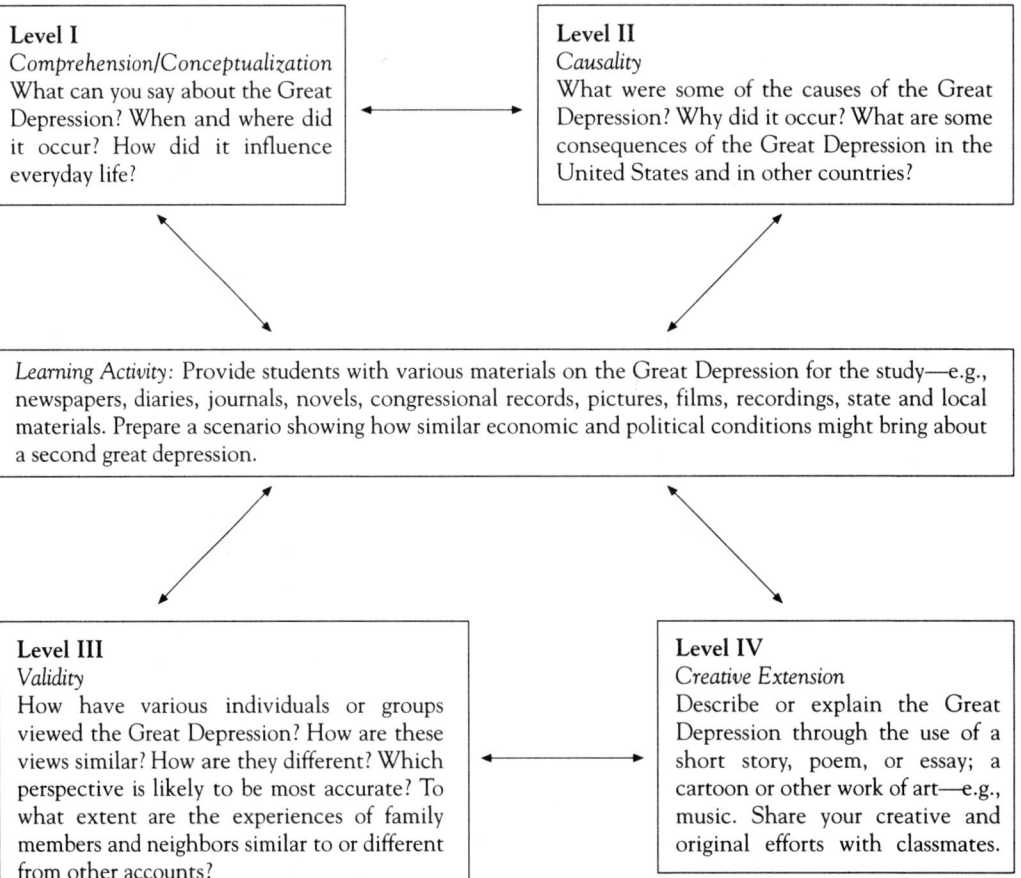

Fig. 2. The Great Depression (Secondary)

At level three, the teacher and students investigate the truth or *validity* of the claims made by historians, economists, journalists, politicians, and family members as to why the depression occurred as well as explanations for its aftermath. The nature of the evidence for each claim is evaluated and the bias of each authority is made explicit.

At the fourth level, students are encouraged to *create* their own questions, interpretation, story, or explanation and to apply or deal with potential *extensions* between the studied depression and other fluctuations in the business cycle before and after the 1930s.

A diagram that links the learning activity to the four levels of inquiry is shown in figure 2. The activity and modes of inquiry are interconnected and may move back and forth between levels.

The authors have provided a similar diagram using the concept of community which is a major concept in most elementary social studies programs. As with any diagram or model, other concepts or topics could be used that enable students to learn and practice the skills of social inquiry. We believe these examples will enable social studies teachers to help students develop and practice various inquiry-related skills (see figure 3).

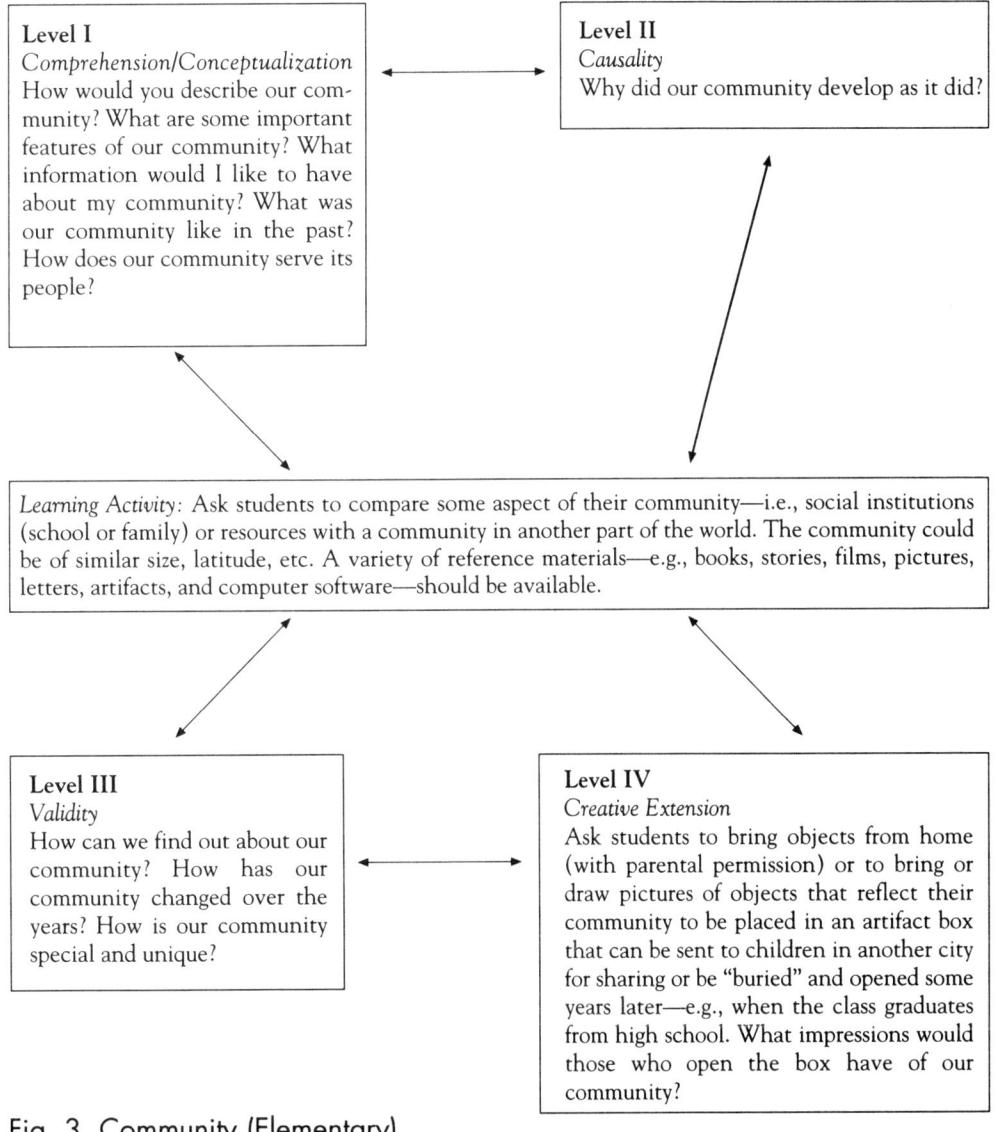

Fig. 3. Community (Elementary)

It should be clear that if students can be motivated and instructed to move comfortably (within an environment that values inquiry) through these four levels, they will have a better chance to develop higher-order thinking primarily because they will have an *opportunity to study the nature of a discipline from several different vantage points.* These experiences should enhance students' reasoning and thinking as they encounter new disciplines, topics, problems, or issues.

Activities that help students conceptualize, deal with causality, validate various claims, and pursue an independent and creative course of action should help enlighten individual and group behavior. Within the classroom, students should have the opportunity to use on a regular basis all four categories of social inquiry. Activities within these areas will "force" students to become more active learners, to ask questions, and to research information by using a variety of data and study the findings of several authorities. This does not suggest a rigid sequence of activities. It does mean that the categories or levels of inquiry are interrelated, and although the order of presentation or involvement of students is somewhat arbitrary, all levels should be used and the model should be thought of as a system or network. All of this takes place, of course, within a context (class, school) that is in the process of becoming a better community where all members are respected, where there is a conscious effort to develop standards of ethics (justice) and aesthetics (craft, quality, excellence), and where the development of meaning in the personal lives of its members is a top priority of instruction.

Social Inquiry and Skills

A few words about the relationship between social inquiry and skills. We might ask what skills should be taught within each of the four (comprehension, causality, validity, and creative extension) categories of the model. Are there skills that could be suggested to help us teach conceptualizing, developing strategies for detecting cause and effect relationships, and discerning the validity of truth claims? The answer is yes *and* no. There certainly are skills, but social inquiry and higher-order thinking come before, as well as after, "skill development" and a pedagogical focus on skills per se may detract from our goal of developing social inquiry and higher-order thinking and actually hinder our effectiveness.

It might be useful to look at a metaphor that can help us see the unity of this model (Hartoonian 1980). Consider the sport of basketball, or the activity of flying an airplane, or any other skillful task in which people engage. Basketball players, for example, learn many different skills —shooting, passing, dribbling, pivoting, and so forth. Coaches spend many hours drilling these often separate skills into their players. But basketball, like any complex human activity, is a "mind game." Players have to reason through a series of decision options and make choices as accurately and as rapidly as possible. They are confronted with an infinite variety of problems to be solved, all within a particular context. Their ability as players is measured not so much in their execution of skills as in their ability to make appropriate decisions. The "game" player, as opposed to the "practice" player, is one who puts skills together in meaningful behavior that helps improve skills, understands the subtleties of the game, and allows the opportunity to become a better and more creative player.

Perhaps the most that we can say about the development of social inquiry and higher-order thinking is that, if we intend that students become better thinkers, then it is important that they be in touch with persons who think with exactness, refinement, and clarity. Teachers should encourage students to be avid readers of the best content (authors), writers of reflective essays, and critics of social phenomena. Awareness and use of the relationships among social studies content, higher-order thinking, and context (school setting) can help us consider the quality of this intercourse, and that quality will be our best guide for developing reflective social inquiry.

Program Sequence: Major Content Focus

Many social studies scope-and-sequence models recommend a spiral or expanding-horizon content approach, starting with the immediate, familiar, and concrete environment in the primary grades and moving outward to the more distant and abstract in high school. The design outlined in figure 4 is a somewhat similar organizational pattern except that its content focus is organized on the basis of grade-level clusters developed around the ten major curriculum themes suggested above. Teachers are encouraged to talk with one another across and within grade-level clusters about social studies content, concepts, abilities, and values.

In organizing the curriculum within each grade-level cluster, students and teachers are asked to address a series of broad content focus questions that allow gathering, integrating, and interpreting data from multiple sources, developing higher-order thinking, and making reasoned judgments about such findings.

The suggested questions can be used to construct content and identify key concepts and topics for the K-12 instructional program. Further, these questions can be used to encourage students and teachers to become active inquirers seeking to find answers or solutions, however tentative, to these questions, issues, concerns, and topics. Teachers and students are urged to grapple intellectually with these questions to facilitate learning for both the teachers and students (Wisconsin Department of Public Instruction 1986). Both students and teachers need to model thinking and explain why they responded as they did. Teachers need to talk about how they came to the conclusions they did and, if they change their conclusions, explain how and why they changed their ideas and opinions based on the acquisition of new knowledge. At the same time, students and teachers need to be open to new ideas and information as they become available.

The grade-level clusters are organized with the focus shown in figure 4.

Grade Level	Content Focus
Primary Grades (K-2)	My Orientation to the World
Intermediate Grades (3-5)	Expanding My World Horizons
Middle School Grades (6-8)	Viewing the World from Different Perspectives
Secondary Grades (9-12)	Assuming Full Citizenship in a Changing World

Fig. 4. Grade-level clusters

Within each of the grade-level clusters, illustrative examples of broad focus questions representing the ten themes are used to organize the curriculum. Naturally, many other questions could be posed and numerous related questions could be formulated within each of the broad question categories. The choice of questions to be used in determining content is the responsibility of the local curriculum committee.

In the following section, the authors briefly identify key characteristics of learners at various grade levels and offer several illustrative examples of student activities to encourage active learning and skill development. We do not, then, answer questions such as, should Mexico or Latin America be taught in the 5th or 6th grade? We believe that in truth it does not make much difference. The important thing to keep in mind is that we must teach substantive content and that it must be current, accurate, and comprehensive. Grade-level assignments of topics are important, as they provide for the elimination of gaps and overlaps in the scope and sequence; but a curriculum plan is a good deal more. A curriculum plan is fundamentally a way for teachers to communicate with one another and the larger community as well.

The Learner and Curriculum Content

Primary Students (Grades K-2)

Students in the primary grades bring to social studies classes a variety of previous experiences that form the foundations for learning and for their intellectual, social, emotional, and physical growth. The social studies program at these grades should enable students to move from a largely egocentric view of the world and develop an understanding of their roles and responsibilities in their families, at school, and in various social institutions and settings.

In these grades, it is important to provide a variety of meaningful, firsthand, concrete learning experiences that draw upon experiences from the home, school, neighborhood, and the world beyond. For example, opportunities should be provided that allow students to develop social participation skills through committee work, role-playing, creative dramatics, greeting classroom visitors, classroom discussion, and informational interviews; to practice research skills by gathering and recording information from various sources such as films, pictures, stories, music, and field trips; to develop citizenship skills through sharing, by accepting responsibility for their own actions through cooperative planning, making compromises, resolving conflicts, and making decisions; and to enhance communication skills through drawing, reading, writing, listening, and speaking activities.

Within this grade-level cluster, students need to have opportunities for individual as well as group learning activities. Appropriate to their maturity level, students should be introduced to concepts and values from the several social studies disciplines through varied concrete learning experiences that will lead to active citizenship participation. There should be numerous opportunities to celebrate and take pride in our cultural heritage by focusing on state, national, and ethnic holidays included in the social studies curriculum.

My Orientation to the World

What can I learn about myself when learning about other people?

Who am I?

What can I learn about myself? What is expected of me?

What is a friend? How can I be friends with both girls and boys? How can I be a friend with older persons? What can we share? What games do I play?

How can I be a good citizen? What are good citizenship practices? What are good habits?

What responsibilities do I have at home, at school, and in my neighborhood?

Why do we need rules at home, at school, and in my neighborhood to limit what we do? What rights do I have?

How can I describe my environment at home, school, and in my neighborhood? How do these environments change?

How do music and the arts influence our environment?

What is a family? How are families alike? How are they different? What are the main functions of families?

Where did my family come from? What family traditions and events do we celebrate in my family?

What are families like in other parts of the world? How can we describe them? What are some customs and traditions celebrated by families around the world? What are some words I know from other languages?

How can I meet my basic needs? What goods and services are available to me?

Why do some people have so much and others have so little? Is this fair?

How do I depend on others? How can I help others?

How do people work with the environment when building a community?

What physical features influence the building of different communities, including our own community?

How can the use of numbers help me make decisions?

How can the use of numbers help me describe families, schools, or neighborhoods?

Who are some community helpers? What are some jobs that can be done by women? by men? by either?

What can I do to help ensure peace at home, at school, and in my neighborhood?

How has technology changed the way I live compared to the way my parents and grandparents lived when they were my age?

What social concepts can I learn through creative dramatics, stories, art, and music? Or through physical education and games?

What ideals or principles can I learn from stories about the past?

Intermediate Students (Grades 3-5)

The social studies curriculum for this grade-level cluster provides an opportunity for interdisciplinary study of our community, state, and nation, with attention given to our culture, environment, people, challenges, and successes. By studying the community, state, and nation, students have the opportunity to learn such concepts as diversity, environment, migration, urbanization, transportation, heritage, ethnicity, technology, beliefs, and others, as well as institutional variables such as family, government, economy, and education in selected settings at various times and in different cultures that provide foundations for ongoing learning.

Students should explore a variety of print and nonprint resources to learn about their cultural, geographic, economic, political, and historical heritage. Most students also enjoy reading and studying the biographies of great and common women and men in various geographical and historical settings. Children's literature, music, and art provide opportunities to integrate social studies with other aspects of the school program. Other excellent sources for data include field trips to museums, historic sites, local businesses, agricultural centers, governmental agencies, and environmental areas. Students also enjoy hearing guest speakers tell about exciting topics in an interesting manner, perhaps with the use of artifacts or other visuals.

Students in these grades need to have numerous activities, experiences, and opportunities to refine and develop previously learned skills and to develop new learning skills, including inquiry and research skills from ever-widening sources to develop critical-thinking and problem-solving abilities. Numerous opportunities for meaningful, individualized, small-group, and entire-group instruction should be offered throughout the year so that students have the opportunity to develop knowledge and skills needed for productive living and learning.

Expanding My World Horizons

How do communities help people meet their basic needs? What goods and services are produced in our community and state?

What features do our community and state have that make them unique and special?

How do communities show diversity? How are communities similar? How have communities changed over time?

What are the characteristics of a good community? A good citizen? How can I be a good citizen?

How are components of culture reflected in our community, state, and nation?

How do our community, state, and nation rely on other parts of the world?

What are some important documents that have shaped our history? How have they influenced our past and our present way of life?

How have women and men influenced our history and the reporting and writing of history?

What are some examples of the contributions of ethnic and cultural groups in our community, state, and nation?

What are some special geographic features of our landscape? What physical features influence the location of communities around the world?

How has technology changed the way we live? How is technology likely to help shape our future?

How can numeric data help us understand changes in history and in our present environment?

What changes are likely to take place in our country and the world in the 21st century?

How do ideas, people, and products circulate in our community, state, and nation? How do people in our region interact with people in other regions?

How has the past shaped our traditions, customs, heritage, attitudes, and values? What can we learn about our society from the study of others?

How did the present come to be as we know it today?

How do laws provide for political, economic, and social stability and control in our daily lives?

Why is there so much political, economic, and social instability in the world? How might we bring stability to the world?

What are some ways to resolve conflicts between individuals, groups, and nations?

Middle School Students (Grades 6-8)

Middle school students are at an age of transition that includes rapid physical growth, intellectual development from the concrete to the more abstract, and social and emotional change as they move from childhood to adolescence. They begin to see themselves and the world around them in different ways. The social studies curriculum for these students is critical because students begin to form their own values, life views, and modes of living, and begin to come to grips with the many complexities of adolescence and adulthood. The development of a positive self-concept is critical because strong peer pressure is a major influence in their lives. They need to develop a healthy respect for self and others in our rapidly changing pluralistic world (Carnegie Council on Adolescent Development 1989).

It is important that the social studies curriculum include topics that engage students' interest as well as extend their context for learning to regions of the earth to gain a global perspective. Students can begin to understand situations from other perspectives and recognize the right of others to express differing points of view. Learning activities should be varied because of the short attention span of students; they should include both physical and social involvement, such as role-playing and simulations, and should involve both inquiry and didactic teaching and learning.

It is also useful to integrate social studies content with art, music, literature, science, mathematics, and environmental studies. Interdisciplinary content and multi-team teaching are becoming more commonplace at those grades than they were in the past. The use of a variety of media can serve as sources of both motivation and information. They assist students in making connections and linkages to their world of here and now and to the rest of the world.

Viewing the World from Different Perspectives

How can content from the social studies provide different perspectives when we study events, institutions, and people around the world?

Where can I find and how can I use numeric information about political, social, and economic institutions?

How can we use numeric data to make decisions in our personal lives?

What is culture? How are cultural regions similar and how are they different? What are some issues, crises, and opportunities facing each culture region at present? How might they be resolved?

What is the social nature of human beings? How do leaders exercise power and authority? How have leaders shaped the course of history? How have common people contributed to our well-being? What roles have women played in the creation and development of culture?

What values are important to our culture? How are these values used in personal and national policy-making?

How does the perception we have of ourselves as individuals and as a nation influence the way we behave toward one another?

What is the nature of the earth and its environment today? How will we "protect" space?

How have world regions become increasingly specialized in the production of certain goods, thereby forming systems of economic networks?

What is the nature of our democratic government at the local, state, and national levels? What are some key features of our government?

What roles have people of color played in the development of the United States?

What efforts are made to recognize and appreciate cultural diversity in our country?

What legal rights and responsibilities do individuals and groups have in our country and in other countries?

How has the United States responded to the many challenges facing our country throughout its history?

What challenges does our nation face in the coming years? How might the nation respond?

What relationships exist between the United States and other areas of the globe? How have these relationships changed over the years?

What common challenges are faced by people around the world? How are they likely to respond to ensure our survival on earth?

How has technology influenced our life-styles, values, and expectations? How might technology shape our lives in the 21st century? How have technological developments changed the lives of people around the world? How has technology changed the ways persons and nations view the world and respond to events?

How might peace be achieved within and among the cultures of the world?

High School Students (Grades 9-12)

Social studies in grades 9-12 should include the opportunity to study in depth (1) our national heritage in a global setting through the study of history, economics, and government; (2) other nations, cultures, and environments of the Western and non-Western world by studying content and concepts from economics, history, geography, and anthropology;

and (3) other social science disciplines through synoptic, behavioral, or analytic studies. Ideally, students will be required to take a social studies course during each of their years in high school and have the opportunity for instruction in at least one course that focuses on synoptic, behavioral, and analytic studies. Examples of social studies course offerings appear in figure 5.

Synoptic Studies	Behavioral Studies	Analytic Studies
Humanities	Anthropology	Economics
Philosophy	Community Service	Environmental Issues
Religious Studies	Futuristic Studies	Law-Related Education
Science, Technology & Society	Ethnic Studies	Political Science/ Government
World Geography/ Global Studies	Human Development	Social Mathematics
History, U.S. World, and U.S. within	Psychology	
World History	Sociology	
	Social Issues of Teenage Life	
	Women's Studies	

Fig. 5. Social studies course offerings

Social studies instruction should include both descriptive and procedural knowledge of the several social sciences disciplines. Critical and creative thinking and problem-solving activities should be emphasized to enable students to gather and weigh data from several sources, to make judgments, and to formulate conclusions. Teachers need to pose questions that will promote genuine classroom discussion and allow for the development of inductive, deductive, analogic, and evaluative thinking skills.

Classroom methodology needs to be varied to account for different learning styles, abilities, talents, and interests of the students. High school students should be provided with opportunities to develop and apply previously learned academic and social-participation skills to new content by examining critical issues in detail from different perspectives. Active learning is encouraged as is direct involvement in the community through such activities as community service, surveying people on important issues, or volunteering to work for a political candidate. A wide range of instructional materials including electronic data bases should be available for student and teacher reference that encourage learning to learn and promote lifelong education.

Assuming Full Citizenship in a Changing World

How has geography influenced the development of human societies?

How do the histories and cultures of various Western and non-Western societies contribute to our understanding of the world today?

What are the major philosophical, religious, economic, and political ideas of our society? How do they help to explain a worldview?

What are some important values that people in various nations and cultures throughout the world hold?

How have the forces of nationalism, industrialism, imperialism, militarism, revolution, technology, and others brought about changes in the attitudes, values, and actions for people in both the Western and non-Western world?

What has democracy contributed to the world? What are some major characteristics of our government and economic system and those of other nations?

How can the histories of the United States and Western civilization be understood as interrelated?

How do people participate actively in political and economic processes and decision making to ensure political, social, and economic justice?

How do the media, government, and private industry use statistical data to inform the public? How can these data be misleading?

What happens when different groups of people come in contact with one another? How have cultural differences led to conflict? How has cultural diffusion benefited humankind?

What major social, political, economic, cultural, scientific, and technological changes have occurred in the United States and elsewhere in the world since World War II? What effects have these changes had on us as individuals, as a nation, and as members of the global community of humankind?

How might these changes influence our values, expectations, and life-styles?

What will our planet Earth be like in the coming years and decades?

How might civil wars and international conflicts be eliminated? How might world peace be achieved?

How can we achieve peace within ourselves? How can we help others achieve peace?

What moral, ethical, and legal obligations do we have toward other human beings and our environment?

What economic, political, humanitarian, and moral roles do international organizations play?

How have civil liberties been gained and how are they protected?

How can human rights be gained and protected for all?

Why has there been tension and conflict between and among various minority groups in the United States and elsewhere around the world? How have rising expectations of minority groups brought about change? What challenges remain to be resolved?

How have changes in societies' expectations, values, and life-styles influenced the role of women and the opportunities available to women at present and in coming years?

How can citizens serve their schools and the larger community? What is the good citizen? What is the good person? What is the good society?

Evaluation

Evaluation is one of three major components of teaching, which are planning the program, deciding instructional strategies, and evaluating student learning. Evaluation helps teachers respond to two important questions: (1) "How do we know whether we have met our instructional objectives?" (2) "How do we know whether we are making a difference in students' lives by our encounters with them?" Of these three components, evaluation most often receives the least attention and is perceived by teachers as difficult and burdensome.

Evaluating Student Learning in Social Studies

Evaluation needs to be kept in mind when planning instruction (selecting content and concepts), identifying objectives, determining skills, deciding teaching and learning strategies, making needed adjustments, and making decisions about students.

In general, four important assumptions are involved in evaluating student outcomes.

- The first assumption is that an outcome measure represents a reasonable and nontrivial sample of student competence in dealing with the most important ideas, skills, processes, and attitudes chosen from the information taught and learned in the lesson or unit.

- The second assumption is that it is reasonable to expect the majority of students in the class to demonstrate increased knowledge and skills because instructional procedures appropriate for the majority of students have been used. It is important to keep in mind that in large classes it is difficult to adapt instruction to take into account most of the individual differences among students when considering their variations in background information, level of interest, and reading and communication skills.

- The third assumption is that the use of both quantitative data and narrative information from several sources corroborate each other, which strengthens the evaluation design.

- The fourth assumption is that student evaluation should be based with equal weight upon common course learnings and on individual and small-group study projects that reflect students' interests.

Evaluating Social Studies Programs

Program evaluation is a process of establishing an ideal program model, collecting data on the present program, and analyzing these data to provide a basis for documenting and making systematic judgments about the strengths and weaknesses of the several program components according to agreed-upon criteria that can help us move toward the established ideal program.

The following questions related to program evaluation help to define conditions and criteria useful for social studies program improvement. These questions suggest an ideal that may be well ahead of current practice. If we do not have a vision of an ideal social studies program, it is unlikely we will be able to improve and extend existing practices.

Such illustrative broad-based program evaluation questions might include the following:

- Is the social studies program represented by an effective K-12 social studies curriculum committee?

- Have social studies goals been established that address the needs of students and society and make available a knowledge of history and the social science disciplines necessary for enlightened citizenship? Are these goals consistent with the overall philosophy and goals of the school?

- Is there a basic social studies requirement for each year for all students enrolled in school? Is there a balanced program that shows the interrelationship between and among the several social science disciplines? Does the social studies program include a study of the relationships among the United States, global themes, and the social science disciplines?

- Does the social studies curriculum program include the district philosophy, goals, and objectives; social studies goals and objectives; social studies scope and sequence; identification and listing of key concepts, skills, and attitudes; evaluation procedures to assess student achievement and the local curriculum; and identification of relevant print and nonprint resources for students and teachers?

- Are activities structured to increase the level of awareness in the community for the accomplishments and needs of the social studies curriculum?

Tied closely to program evaluation are a number of questions that need to be asked concerning staff development opportunities for social studies teachers. Such questions should include the following:

- What staff development opportunities are available to social studies teachers?
- What opportunities are provided for teachers to have renewing or broadening professional experiences for curriculum work and program development?
- In what manner does the administration supervise curriculum and instruction in the social studies?
- To what extent are teachers given time to visit one another's classes or other schools and discuss methods and materials used?
- To what extent are teachers involved in selecting new instructional programs and materials? How are instructional materials selected? Have appropriate guidelines been established?
- What percentage of the staff belongs to and is active in the local, state, and national social studies professional organizations?
- How frequently and with what support are teachers encouraged to attend conferences, workshops, or other professional meetings?
- What is the nature of the social studies professional library? Do teachers have access to current professional literature in social studies education, the social science disciplines, and other related areas?
- What contributions are teachers making to the school or district social studies program, and to the larger social studies community of scholars?

Settings for Learning in Social Studies

As with all parts of the curriculum, the learning environment must be conducive to the teaching and learning process. The classroom environment should be such that students are willing to take risks by seeking and sharing information and in trying out new ideas. Within the classroom, there should be numerous opportunities for positive student-to-student, student-to-teacher, and teacher-to-teacher interactions as well as opportunities for students and teachers to make choices. Within the classroom (and in the media center), there should be a rich variety of student and teacher resources and instructional materials. There should be opportunities to use the newer technologies, including computers and interactive video in searching for information and in learning.

The physical arrangement of the classroom should encourage interaction and cooperative learning. The classroom should facilitate individual and both small- and large-group learning and provide for variety to promote active learning. Attention should also be given to aesthetics that may facilitate or hinder student learning.

It is also important to recognize that learning extends beyond the walls and boundaries of the school into the larger community. Each of these social institutions influences learning: family, home, church, community, and media, as does socioeconomic status. Students should come to recognize that learning takes place in multiple settings—e.g., while walking to school; traveling with family members; reading a book or magazine; viewing an event or listening to a presentation personally or vicariously; attending a concert or dramatic performance; or engaging in comparative shopping. Obviously learning should be encouraged in various contexts and settings.

Whatever the setting for learning, it is important that students and teachers recognize there is a social contract in operation and this contract needs to address such concepts as fairness, justice, participation, and integrity; and provide for an honest study of real issues.

Conclusion

Because of growth in the creation of information and knowledge, an intriguing concept has now been applied to the area of knowing. That concept is the *half-life of knowledge*. For example, the half-life of an engineering degree is now said to be four years or less. What is the half-life of a newly developed curriculum for the social studies? It is not very long, and so we need, as never before, to place additional emphasis upon professional growth, communication among colleagues, and the development of a school climate that will facilitate ongoing curriculum development and experimentation. These components of development include a sustainable and planned program of curriculum implementation, evaluation, revision, and professional development that will allow teachers, administrators, students, and community members the opportunity to examine and talk about curriculum in precise ways.

This would mean that the responsibility for the knowledge, concepts, skills, and values taught within the K-12 social studies program would be placed more directly on members of the local staff—a staff with the mandate and resources (empowerment) to carry out the ongoing development of the curricular and instructional programs. Further, attention would be placed upon the relationship of the school with the larger community, as students should have opportunities to serve their community and learn firsthand about its social, political, and economic cultures and environments.

Finally, it must be stated and restated that curriculum is fundamentally a matter of communication. Thus the real purpose of a scope-and-sequence design is to serve as a grammar or metalanguage that professionals can use as they talk about their craft. In a sense, a scope and sequence can be arbitrary. What cannot be arbitrary, or without structure, is the common language of the professional that allows for criticism, freedom, and growth within a community of scholars. These actions can bring a degree of congruency between our professional principles and school practices.

Michael Hartoonian is Supervisor of Social Studies Education for the Wisconsin Department of Public Instruction and an adjunct professor in the Department of Curriculum and Instruction at the University of Wisconsin-Madison; Margaret Laughlin is an Associate Professor in Education at the University of Wisconsin-Green Bay.

References

Bradley Commission on History in Schools. *Building a History Curriculum: Guidelines for Teaching History in Schools.* Washington, D.C.: The Educational Excellence Network, 1988.

Bragaw, D.H., and H.M. Hartoonian. "Social Studies: The Study of People in Society." In *Content of the Curriculum*, ed. Ronald S. Brandt. Alexandria, Va.: Association for Supervision and Curriculum Development, 1988.

Curriculum Task Force of the National Commission on Social Studies in Schools and the National Social Science Disciplinary Associations. *Charting a Course: Social Studies Curriculum for the 21st Century.* (Draft.) Washington, D.C.: Curriculum Task Force of the National Commission on Social Studies in Schools and the National Social Science Disciplinary Associations, 1989.

Danto, A.C. *Analytical Philosophy of History.* London: Cambridge University Press, 1965.

Dewey, J. *Democracy and Education.* New York: Macmillan, 1916.

Gagnon, Paul. *Democracy's Untold Story: What World History Textbooks Neglect.* Washington, D.C.: Education for Democracy Project of the American Federation of Teachers, 1987.

Gilliard, June V., Jean Caldwell, Bruce R. Dalgaard, Robert Highsmith, Robert Reinke, and Michael Watts. *Economics: What and When Scope and Sequence Guidelines, K-12.* (Master Curriculum Guide in Economics.) New York: Joint Council on Economic Education, 1988.

Hartoonian, H.M. "Reasoning as a Metaphor for Skill Development in the Social Studies Curriculum." *Theory and Research in Social Education* 7, no. 4 (1980).

Joint Committee on Geographic Education. *Guidelines for Geographic Education: Elementary and Secondary Schools.* Washington, D.C., and Macomb, Ill.: Association of American Geographers and the National Council for Geographic Education, 1984.

Task Force on Education of Young Adolescents. *Turning Points: Preparing American Youth for the 21st Century.* New York: Carnegie Corporation of New York, 1989.

Tuchman, Barbara W. *A Distant Mirror: The Calamitous 14th Century.* New York: Ballantine, 1978; xix-xx.

Wisconsin Department of Public Instruction. *A Guide to Curriculum Planning in Social Studies.* Bulletin No. 6251, 1986. Wisconsin Department of Public Instruction, P.O. Box 7841, Madison, Wisconsin 53707.

Note: Several states and local school districts have developed social studies curriculum frameworks and guides in recent years. It is wise to be knowledgeable about state curriculum efforts and those of other related social studies groups.

Additional Readings

Bartlett, F. *Thinking: An Experimental and Social Study.* London: George Allen and Unwin, 1958.

Chance, P. *Thinking in the Classroom.* New York: Teachers College Press, Columbia University, 1986.

Glaser, R. "Education and Thinking: The Role of Knowledge." *American Psychologist* 39 (1984).

Hartoonian, H.M. "The First 'R'—Reasoning." *Social Studies* 71, no. 4 (1980).

Hirsch, E. D., Jr. "Cultural Literacy." *American Scholar* 52 (Spring 1983).

Mayer, R.E. *Thinking and Problem Solving: An Introduction to Human Cognition and Learning.* Glenview, Ill.: Scott, Foresman, 1977.

McPeck, J.E. *Critical Thinking in Education.* New York: St. Martin's Press, 1981.

Newmann, F.M. "Higher Order Thinking in High School Social Studies: An Analysis of Classroom, Teachers, Students, and Leadership." Madison: National Center on Effective Secondary Schools, University of Wisconsin, 1988.

Reitman, W. *Cognition and Thought.* New York: Wiley, 1985.

Smith, F. *Comprehension and Learning: A Conceptual Framework for Teachers.* New York: Holt, Rinehart and Winston, 1975.

Toulmin, S. *The Uses of Argument.* London: Cambridge University Press, 1958.

Wertheimer, M. *Productive Thinking.* New York: Harper, 1959.

Social Studies within a Global Education

Willard M. Kniep

The scope and sequence presented here are rooted in global education, an approach to schooling reflecting a belief that there is a critical need for schools to prepare young people for life in a world increasingly characterized by pluralism, interdependence, and change. This movement gains new momentum as political leaders and policymakers, as well as educators at all levels, join the call for global education. Typical is the 1989 report of the National Governors' Association which cites the need for making education more responsive to a changing world:

> Times have changed. Revolutionary advances in science, technology, communications, and transportation have brought nations and peoples together. World trade and financial, economic, and political developments have transformed disparate economic systems into a highly interdependent global marketplace. Today, the nations that inhabit the planet are often more closely linked than neighboring states or villages were at the turn of the century.
>
> Yet these important changes are not reflected in the way many U.S. schools prepare students for citizenship. In educating students, the languages, cultures, values, traditions, and even the location of other nations are often ignored. Schools and universities reflect the same lack of global understanding that pervades the nation from government and business leaders to school children.

In this approach to schooling, educating for citizenship remains the central mission of schools. However, it extends the view of citizenship since, in today's world, citizenship increasingly includes participation not only in the community, state, and nation but in the global community as well. This view is rooted in two realities that have become more and more apparent since the end of World War II.

First, today as never before, all human beings live in a multiboundary world, not simply a world of nation-states, but one with a diversity of worldwide systems in which all people affect and are affected by others around the globe. Second, humanity is increasingly threatened by problems that cannot be solved by actions taken only at the national level. For a number of our most pressing environmental and social problems—contamination of the environment, warming of the atmosphere, world hunger, international terrorism, the nuclear threat—there will either be international solutions or no solutions at all.

Within a global education, social studies continue with a specific mandate and special responsibility for providing citizenship education. Their purpose is to equip all students to become effective participants in shaping our nation's future by giving them the knowledge and skills to arrive at informed judgments; by strengthening their commitment to democratic values and processes; and by making it possible for them to participate responsibly in the world in which they live.

Within our democracy, the judgments of citizens are the ultimate source of policy and action. In our history, these judgments have provided not only legitimation for decisions made by leaders but have frequently led our leaders. The goals of social studies, then, must be derived from the requirements of citizenship in a democratic society that is one of the most dominant and powerful actors in today's interdependent world.

Our nation is robust and energetic, and our culture influences—for better or worse—the entire world. Our dominance of the international economy and our high standard of living both depend on and affect peoples and nations in all parts of the earth. This extraordinary position, and the privileges and responsibilities it implies for U.S. citizenship, must be reflected in our definition of the social studies.

The content of social studies is drawn from history, the social sciences, and, to some extent, from the humanities and natural sciences. But we must also acknowledge the contributions of other, sometimes new and often interdisciplinary, fields to what we know about the contemporary world—fields like journalism, future studies, policy studies, development studies, and environmental studies. Furthermore, we should emphasize the interdisciplinary nature of social studies itself, since the future is likely to require more integrative thinking and interdisciplinary problem solving, not less.

The way we teach must reflect the experience and development of our learners. But even more important to achieving our citizenship goals, we must place our students actively in the center of the learning process. If students are to think globally as they act locally, if they are to be actively at the center of their world, and if they are to be engaged with what we want them to learn, then social studies must be taught in ways that make learning active, interactive, hands-on, and engaging.

Goals

Knowledge

The 1979 Social Studies Curriculum Guidelines envisioned three particular functions for the knowledge component of the curriculum: to provide a historical perspective, to help a person perceive patterns and systems, and to provide the foundation for social participation.

That vision is still valid today. In a global education, the historical perspective will include a grasp of the evolution of universal human values and unique worldviews, the historical development of contemporary global systems, and the antecedent conditions and causes of today's global issues and problems. The systems perspective will enable students to see themselves, their communities, and their nation as actors in and on economic, political, ecological, and technological systems extending throughout the globe. Knowledge as a basis for social participation must include not only historical and systems perspectives but an understanding of the causes, effects, and potential solutions for the great problems and issues of our time.

Abilities

An important goal of the social studies is to help students develop the skills and abilities that citizens need to make informed judgments. However, it is important that we state these goals in the context of our other goals and pursue them holistically in our curricula. To do so creates a reason and need for our students to develop and use them as a natural part of meaningful study. To do otherwise not only violates the principle of wholeness that is basic to global education but perpetuates the false dichotomy between content and process that has plagued the social studies.

Among the most important of our goals is the development of abilities associated with developing a global perspective. These include identifying perspectives, seeing patterns, tracing linkages and cause-and-effect relationships, and expanding the repertoire of choice in solving problems.

A second important goal in this domain is to help students develop and refine the intellectual capacities often associated with critical thinking. We must remember, however, that students come to us, without exception, with the capacity to think and reason. From infancy they have engaged in critical thinking as they have seen and analyzed relationships, applied information to new situations, made predictions, synthesized information from multiple sources, and formed judgments based on what they know. Our goal should be to engage and expand these intellectual capacities by providing opportunity, significant content, and engaging context to do so.

A third goal is to help students develop skills for inquiry and learning. Social studies have a special responsibility for helping students develop skill in using the tools of scientific inquiry as modeled by social scientists and historians. By their very nature, they must require students to gather data through observation, interviews, surveys, and reading; organize data using charts, maps, models, field notes, and other tools; and communicate what is learned through a variety of forms of expression.

Valuing

Values are embedded in the content we choose, in the teaching and learning processes we employ, and in the structure of social and physical environments. Our choices in these areas should be guided by our goals.

A primary goal of social studies should be that students develop perspectives, concerns, tendencies, and standards for their role as citizens of a democratic society in an interdependent world. If our programs are successful, students' perspectives will help them see their linkages to others and the common humanity of all people; their concerns will be for life, human rights, individual responsibility, and ecological balance; their tendencies will be toward participation, collaboration, acceptance of diversity, and peaceful resolution of conflict; and their standards will include justice, equity, self-determination, individual freedoms, human dignity, and honesty.

The content that we select should ground students in a basic knowledge of the values of their own cultures and society and should engage them in examining the values of others to see the commonality and diversity among humanity. Both the processes we employ and the social and physical structures we put in place must model in microcosm the values we affirm.

Social Participation

To claim citizenship education as the central focus and mandate of the social studies, we must identify social participation as our central goal. As the 1979 guidelines assert, the knowledge, abilities, and values in social studies programs come to fruition in social participation.

The goal of social studies should be to equip students for responsible and effective participation in all the systems in which they live. In the best of all possible worlds, as a result of their social studies programs students would participate in democratic institutions knowing how and why they work, with full awareness of the rights and responsibilities that go with participation. Furthermore, students would be led to economic decisions that maximize individual and social benefits—knowing that these decisions are dependent on and have consequences for others around the world—and to life-style decisions that contribute to personal well-being and pleasure with consideration for social and ecological benefits and costs.

Ultimately, social studies programs must empower students to participate. That is, students must see that they have a role in making the world a safer, more just, and equitable place for all humanity. It is not enough simply to know about persistent problems and issues, nor is it sufficient to be able to think and talk rationally and creatively about alternative solutions and to identify the value dilemmas inherent in them. Education becomes complete only when it moves us and provides us with the means and opportunity to act to affect local, national, and global problems.

Scope and Sequence

The scope of the curriculum should not be limited by tradition or by familiar topics that have always been taught. The determinants should be the purposes that we have set out for social studies, our best analysis of the current realities in which students live, the requirements of citizenship in the 21st century, and an understanding of the basic nature and elements of those realities from the scholarship of history, social science, and other disciplines.

The scope of the social studies curriculum, then, should reflect the present and historical realities of a global society. As a way to bring some order to thinking about those realities, I propose four essential elements of study in a global education that set the boundaries for the scope of the social studies curriculum.

1. **The Study of Systems** including the *economic, political, ecological,* and *technological* systems dominating our interdependent world.
2. **The Study of Human Values**—both *universal values* defining what it means to be human and *diverse values* derived from group membership and contributing to unique world views.
3. **The Study of Persistent Issues and Problems** including *peace and security* issues, national and international *development* issues, local and global *environmental* issues, and *human rights* issues.
4. **The Study of Global History**—focusing on the evolution of universal and diverse human values, the historical development of contemporary global systems, and the antecedent conditions and causes of today's global issues.

In organizing the sequence of the social studies curriculum, every effort should be made to retain the holistic character of global education. Doing so will ensure that students can capture the sense of interdependence characterizing the modern world. Furthermore, the sequence of study should lead to broad and transferable conceptual understanding of patterns and relationships. It must keep students at the center of their learning and their world.

As a way of achieving consistency with these principles, I propose using themes as basic organizers for the social studies curriculum. In the social studies curriculum themes function as a means for focusing attention, for making connections among disparate elements across curricula, and for applying what is learned to the rest of life.

This thematic model uses three types of themes for curriculum organization derived from the structural elements of the disciplines underlying the social studies. Each discipline uses *concepts* for organizing inquiry and for describing its structure and view of reality. Each studies certain *phenomena* that delimit its field of inquiry. Each focuses on *persistent problems* for which its knowledge may provide explanations or solutions.

Conceptual Themes

Work within social studies should be organized, first of all, around concepts: the big ideas forming the mental structures and language that human beings use for thinking about and describing the world. The particular concepts used as curricular themes are characteristically abstract and relational. They are not labels for real, concrete things but generally describe how people, things, and events relate to one another. Such concepts, while shared in people's language and thinking about the world, are idiosyncratic to an extent since they are individually formed and reflect the transaction between persons' prior knowledge and experience and the meaning taken from new experience.

The five conceptual themes, listed and defined in the accompanying box, have been selected as basic curriculum organizers because they are essential to the development of a global perspective. They are metaconcepts in the sense that they consistently appear in the language and thinking of the social and natural sciences and because they serve as organizers around which other concepts tend to cluster.

> Conceptual Themes for the Social Studies
>
> **1. Interdependence:**
> We live in a world of systems in which the actors and components interact to make up a unified, functioning whole.
> *Related concepts:* causation, community, exchange, government, groups, interaction, systems.
>
> **2. Change:**
> The process of movement from one state of being to another is a universal aspect of the planet and is an inevitable part of life and living.
> *Related concepts:* adaptation, cause and effect, development, evolution, growth, revolution, time.
>
> **3. Culture:**
> People create social environments and systems comprised of unique beliefs, values, traditions, language, customs, technology, and institutions as a way of meeting basic human needs; shaped by their own physical environments and contact with other cultures.
> *Related concepts:* adaptation, aesthetics, diversity, languages, norms, roles, values, space, time.
>
> **4. Scarcity:**
> An imbalance exists between relatively unlimited wants and limited available resources necessitating the creation of systems for deciding how resources are to be distributed.
> *Related concepts:* conflict, exploration, migration, opportunity cost, policy, resources, specialization.
>
> **5. Conflict:**
> People and nations often have differing values and opposing goals resulting in disagreement, tensions, and sometimes violence necessitating skill in coexistence, negotiation, living with ambiguity, and conflict resolution.
> *Related concepts:* authority, collaboration, competition, interests/positions, justice, power, rights.

Phenomenological Themes

Topical organization of textbooks and curricula focused on phenomena—people, places, and events—is common in social studies. One of the problems with this approach has been that, by focusing on a single phenomenon such as a nation or region, we may overemphasize uniqueness and differences and ignore similarities and interconnectedness—an outcome that runs directly counter to developing a global perspective. In a global education, phenomenological themes would be selected for their contribution to understanding the world's systems, cultures, and historical evolution.

Phenomenological themes fall in two categories. The first is the *actors and components* playing major roles in the world's systems or within the sphere of human cultures and values. Actors meeting these criteria include specific nations, organizations, religious and cultural groups, significant individuals, and institutions. Components include geographic regions, significant documents, geological features, landforms, and systems and subsystems.

The second category of phenomenological themes is comprised of major *events*. Such events, both historical and contemporary, are selected because of their contribution to the development of contemporary world systems and the evolution of diversity and commonality of human values and cultures.

Specific phenomena are chosen as themes because we are convinced they are essential to students' understanding of the world. Individual choices depend, to a large extent, on the needs and location of students. For students in the United States, knowing the history, roles, and values of their own community, state, and nation is critical to understanding the world's systems and the interaction and evolution of cultures and values. So too, their historical perspective must include the major events in the development of their own country. At the same time, however, students will truly understand the world in which they live only if our choices include the broad range of actors, components, and events that continue to shape the systems, values, and history of our diverse planet.

Persistent Problem Themes

These themes embrace the global issues and problems characterizing the modern world. By engaging with persistent problems, students can clearly see their interdependent nature and how a variety of actors, themselves included, affect the problems and their solutions. The study of persistent problems would be incomplete unless it contributed to an understanding of their historical antecedents and the ways in which problems and their solutions relate to cultural perspectives and human values.

It is possible to generate a lengthy list of specific persistent problems that plague us globally and locally. However, the vast majority of problems seem to fall into the following four categories.

Peace and Security

the arms race
East-West relations
terrorism
colonialism
democracy vs. tyranny

National/International Development

hunger and poverty
overpopulation
North-South relations
appropriate technology
international debt crisis

Environmental Problems

acid rain
pollution of streams
depletion of rain forests
nuclear waste disposal
maintenance of fisheries

Human Rights

apartheid
indigenous homelands
political imprisonment
religious persecution
refugees

Persistent problems, by their very nature, permeate every level of existence—from global to national to local— with their symptoms and causes. Moreover, the solutions to persistent problems will come both through individual behaviors taken collectively and through policy decisions taken multilaterally. Because of this, themes in this category consistently provide opportunities for students to find their role as citizens and develop their abilities for social participation in local versions of global problems or local efforts to alleviate global problems.

Placement of Themes by Grade Level

This curricular model is presented as a tool for use at the local level in generating scope and sequence for social studies. It places the social studies at the center of an overall school program comprising a global education.

The following description of a K-12 social studies curriculum is one example of how a school district might translate the goals and principles of the model into a scope and sequence. It is thus an example of decisions that need to be made by any school district—involving administrators, curriculum specialists, and teachers—in the process of determining what is to be taught, how it is to be taught, and in what order.

The example, in addition to incorporating the goals and elements of the global education model for social studies, is based on several assumptions about human development and learning consistent with the holistic perspective of the model itself.

- Human beings function as whole organisms: thought, speech, emotion, and psychomotor activities occur simultaneously and in concert. Therefore learning is a holistic enterprise in which artificial separation of instruction into content, skills, values, etc., is to be avoided whenever possible.
- Learning is basically an active and interactive process. Methods that cast the learning in a passive role should be used sparingly and avoided wherever possible.
- The younger the learner or the more unfamiliar the subject, the greater the need to provide opportunities for student interaction with concrete examples in instructional sequences.
- Conceptual understanding is built on repeated contact with a variety of real people, places, and events that are exemplars of the concept to be developed.

The example emphasizes the importance of developing a conceptual foundation for understanding the way the world works. In the early years, it gives priority to conceptual themes as a basis for the increasingly specialized study and development of breadth and depth that will take place in later years. The objective is to have students see the pervasive nature of conceptual relationships in all aspects of their world.

The proposed scope and sequence describe the substantive focus of the curriculum, reflecting the assumption that processes and values are inseparable from content and that teaching and learning ought to be holistic enterprises. Methods of teaching will rely heavily on inquiry strategies and scientific processes as means of fostering the ability to understand and describe the world in terms of relationships. Teaching will emphasize hands-on processes that involve students with people, events, and primary resources and will facilitate social participation.

Elementary Program

The elementary program will be implemented primarily through teacher-made thematic units. These units, using the community as a laboratory, are aimed at developing skill in the use of scientific processes by taking advantage of opportunities to make observations, conduct interviews and surveys, and analyze and solve issues and problems. They include a variety of primary source materials, trade books, media, and other resources.

The development of a conceptual foundation is the first priority of the elementary program. Therefore, each of the conceptual themes has been adopted as the organizing focus of study, with increasing levels of sophistication, at several points in the elementary curriculum. The second priority is the development of social participation skills, reflected in the designation of persistent problem themes at each grade, so children will begin to see themselves actively in the role of citizens.

In the early elementary years, the program assigns responsibility for direct instruction related to each of the conceptual themes at specific grade levels. The specific content of units in the early grades has not been specified; teachers will have the opportunity and support to design their own units of instruction. Similarly, persistent problem themes have been assigned to grade levels with the expectation that teachers will design units to engage their students in local manifestations of global problems and issues. These units are to be interdisciplinary whenever possible and themes are to be used to focus and provide a context for work in curricular areas such as writing, literature study, and arithmetic.

Beginning with the middle grades, the social studies program becomes more content-specific. However, the emphasis continues to be on thematic organization of that content. As a result, the program in the middle grades more nearly approximates a course structure while retaining the interdisciplinary potential of the thematic unit.

Following is an abbreviated summary of the program for the elementary grades:

Kindergarten: In the kindergarten program, the conceptual themes will be threaded throughout socialization and structured play activities rather than delivered through formal units of instruction. The emphasis will be on helping children discover the systems in their lives such as the family, the classroom, toys, and machines and on developing an appreciation of the world of similarities and differences. The program will feature manipulatives and hands-on experiences, children's literature, and the use of the school and community as laboratories.

Grade 1: The assigned conceptual themes are *interdependence* and *scarcity*. In the interdependence units, student inquiry will focus on the linkages among people and the roles they assume in social situations such as classrooms, recreational activities, or community workplaces; on the mutual dependencies among living and nonliving things in the natural environment; and on how simple mechanical and biological systems are made up of component parts that work together. The scarcity units will be designed to help students differentiate between wants and needs and to use the economic principle of opportunity cost to analyze their own behavior and the decisions made by households and local businesses.

Within the third assigned theme, *environmental problems*, students will be able to identify examples and causes of pollution and waste within the school and community and to develop alternative solutions for these examples.

Grade 2: The assigned conceptual themes are *change* and *culture*. The highlights of the change units will be for students to identify the persistence of change in themselves and begin to make a record of change for their community and environment, using family members, friends, letters, diaries, newspaper articles, pictures, and other documents as data sources. In the culture units, students will explore the universal aspects of cultures by examining their own cultures and the culture of the classroom and school, and by looking at the cultures of children around the world through artifacts, trade books, films, and other sources.

Development is the assigned problems theme. The focus of inquiry will be hunger and poverty in the community and other parts of the world. An essential part of the units will permit students to decide on and undertake a response to the problem.

Grade 3: The assigned conceptual theme is *conflict*. An extended unit will enable students to recognize conflict situations and their causes and to develop skills in collaborative problem solving and conflict resolution.

In the first phenomenological theme in the program, students will study local *actors in the economic system*. Students will identify the collaborative aspects of local workplaces, markets, and businesses, as well as the interdependence of supply and demand in a competitive marketplace.

The assigned problems theme is *peace and security*. Units will engage students in analyzing current local and global conflicts where the underlying cause is threatened security. Emphasis will be on examining and developing alternative means of conflict resolution.

Grade 4: Study of the state will be organized around selected themes. In state history, students will use the concept of *culture* to analyze the contributions of various groups, beginning with the indigenous peoples, to the development of the state. The study of contemporary life in the state will use the theme of *interdependence* to help students identify the economic, political, cultural, and technological linkages of the state to the rest of the nation and world.

Environmental problems serves as an organizing theme to engage students in inquiry about major environmental concerns of the state.

The program focuses on a phenomenological theme—*system components*—to study the contribution of the state's major landforms, river systems, forests and deserts, and major cities to its quality of life.

Grade 5: Students will study the history of the United States thematically. Rather than being organized chronologically, the program will facilitate a conceptual understanding of United States' development, and will emphasize the components that make it unique among the nations of the world. Conceptually, the history will focus on the historical and contemporary *interdependence* of the United States with the rest of the world, the role of *conflict* in the nation's development, and the economic evolution of the United States in a world of *scarcity*.

Additionally, students will undertake in-depth study of selected components that contribute to the uniqueness of the United States as a nation such as the Constitution, the federal system, and the presidency. The persistent problem of *human rights* will also be a focus as students study the problems and progress of the United States in implementing the basic values of justice, equity, and individual freedoms for all of its citizens.

Grade 6: The concepts of *change*, *culture*, *conflict*, and *interdependence* are used to organize the study of Latin America, Africa, and Asia, including historical and contemporary perspectives. The persistent problem of *Development*, emphasizing the role of the United States and the linkages of its citizens to the developing world will be examined throughout the program.

The Secondary Schools Program

The programs in the Junior High School and Senior High School will shift in focus from the more generalized study of the elementary years to an emphasis on more content-specific study, and will increasingly assume a course format. The program is designed to provide depth and breadth of knowledge of content derived primarily from the adopted scope of the program. That is, the program will aim at increasing knowledge of human values, including those that characterize life in the United States; global systems, including the role of the United States and other major actors; and contemporary global problems and issues. In addition, a high priority is for students to develop a historical perspective that includes the development of the United States and of the interdependence that characterizes today's world.

Grade 7: The program emphasizes a functional knowledge of major global systems. In the first semester, students will examine the global economic system. Beginning with the U.S. economy, the course will stimulate an analysis of major economic systems and the interdependence of the global economy. In the second semester, students will study political systems through a similar approach.

Concurrently, students will be involved in an interdisciplinary course focusing on ecological systems during the first semester and technological systems the second. The course will draw most heavily on the social and natural sciences.

Grade 8: Students will explore the domain of human values, beginning with an analysis of basic values in U.S. society such as individual freedoms and rights, the work ethic, majority rule, and equity. The course will trace the origins of those values from the writings and movements that shaped Western civilization through the founding documents of the United States.

The second part of the program will take a similar approach to other non-Western traditions. First priority in selecting these traditions will be to include major actors in today's world such as Islamic nations, Eastern Europe, and selected countries of Asia, Africa, and Latin America.

In a concurrent course, students will engage in interdisciplinary study, drawing primarily from literature and the humanities, focused on how each of the traditions under study embodies its values in its history of ideas and in art, literature, music, and other forms of aesthetic expression.

Grade 9: The 9th grade will revolve around global history, emphasizing the evolution of the interdependence of the contemporary world through the more or less continuous contact and exchange among civilizations of the past two thousand years. The course will examine the evidence and results of historical contact and exchange among early civilizations and the effects of subsequent migration, exploration, export of technology, colonization, and modern technology. The aim of the course will be to provide a broad historic panorama for interpreting today's international relationships.

Grade 10: Although organized chronologically, this two-semester course in U.S. history will emphasize the relationship of the history of the United States to the history of the globe using conceptual themes as a framework for analysis. The course will also give specific attention to the unique approach of the United States to the problems of development, the environment, human rights, and domestic and international peace and security.

Grade 11: The objects of study will be major actors in the modern world. The course will focus on nation-states as major actors in the global political and economic arenas. Students will compare the approaches of selected nations to persistent problems and will analyze their basic social and political values. The role of other actors—the United Nations, nongovernmental organizations, multinational corporations, unions, and grass-roots movements—will also be analyzed.

Grade 12: The senior year is designed as the capstone of the social studies program, engaging students in applying the themes and substance of the previous years to the study of contemporary global problems and issues. In the first semester, using the conceptual themes as a framework for systems analysis, students will pursue an inquiry project—collecting and analyzing data, drawing conclusions, and developing alternative solutions—resulting in a senior thesis related to the problem of their choice.

In the second semester they will participate in a community project in which they will implement some aspects of their theses. The senior project, undertaken in cooperation with a community-service organization, a political party, or a nonprofit organization will provide students a culminating school-linked opportunity to experience the role of a citizen in a democratic society within a real-world setting.

References

Alger, Chadwick F., and James E. Harf. "Global Education: Why? For Whom? About What?" In *Promising Practices in Global Education*, ed. Robert Freeman. New York: The American Forum, 1987.

America in Transition—The International Frontier: Report of the Task Force on International Education. Washington, D.C.: National Governors' Association, 1989.

Cleveland, Harlan. "The World We're Preparing Our Schoolchildren For." *Social Education* 50 (October 1986): 416-23.

Goodlad, John I. "The Learner at the World's Center." *Social Education* 50 (October 1986):424-36.

Hanvey, Robert G. *An Attainable Global Perspective*. New York: Center for Global Perspectives, 1978.

Kniep, Willard M. "Thematic Units: Revitalizing a Trusted Tool." *The Clearing House* (April 1979): 388-94.

———. "Defining a Global Education by Its Content." *Social Education* 50 (October 1986): 437-45.

———. *Next Steps in Global Education: A Handbook for Curriculum Development*. New York: The American Forum, 1987.

National Council for the Social Studies. "Revision of the NCSS Social Studies Curriculum Guidelines." *Social Education* 43 (April 1979):261-78.

National Council for the Social Studies Task Force on Scope and Sequence. "In Search of a Scope and Sequence for Social Studies." *Social Education* 48 (April 1984): 249-62.

Reischauer, Edwin. *Toward the 21st Century: Education for a Changing World*. New York: Knopf, 1973.

The Study Commission on Global Education. *The United States Prepares for Its Future*. New York: The American Forum, 1987.

Willard M. Kniep is Vice President for Research and Development at The American Forum for Global Education (formerly known as Global Perspectives in Education), 45 John St., Suite 1200, New York, NY 10038.

NCSS Position Statements and Guidelines

Social Studies for Early Childhood and Elementary School Children Preparing for the
  21st Century 73
Essential Characteristics of a Citizenship Education Program 87
Essential Characteristics of a Citizenship Program: Criteria Checklist 88
Global Education 89
Study About Religions in the Social Studies Curriculum 92
Teaching about Science, Technology and Society in Social Studies: Education for
  Citizenship in the 21st Century 94

Social Studies for Early Childhood and Elementary School Children Preparing for the 21st Century

A Report from NCSS Task Force on Early Childhood/Elementary Social Studies*

Approved by NCSS Board of Directors, June 1988

POSITION STATEMENT & GUIDELINES

This position paper will discuss the definition, rationale, and goals for social studies in the early childhood/elementary years; the developmental characteristics that should be considered in planning a social studies program; an overview of the basic research for elementary social studies; a look at the current status of social studies in the elementary school; and a discussion of preservice and inservice education for teachers of early childhood/elementary social studies.

Society is characterized by increasingly rapid social and technological change. Society's ability to orchestrate change frequently outstrips its ability to reflect on the ramifications of what it has done. Are children developing skills to absorb new information in light of the information explosion? Are they learning structures for understanding and adapting to changes in technology, the marketplace, and their own family organization? Are they beginning to learn about interdependence and the relationship of technology to social conditions?

When they leave the classroom, many children do not return immediately to the family setting but go to a day-care facility where they again interact with others from a variety of backgrounds. Nearly all the children spend more hours each week watching television than they spend in any other activity besides sleeping. As they sit passively watching, they are bombarded by messages. They take in spotty, disconnected information about war, the homeless, Ethiopia, the president, and the Soviets. Are they learning any structures for interpreting this information and fitting it into a larger framework? Commercial television networks see children as an economic force and press them to make consumer decisions. Are children learning to evaluate these messages, or do they continue to sit passively as they are manipulated?

The social studies in the early childhood/elementary years are crucial if we expect the young people of this nation to become active, responsible citizens for maintaining the democratic values upon which this nation was established. Unless children acquire the foundations of knowledge, attitudes, and skills in social studies in the important elementary years, it is unlikely that teachers in the junior and senior high schools will be successful in preparing effective citizens for the 21st century.

I. What problems do young children encounter as they enter school?

Consider a kindergarten class in any one of thousands of school systems in the United States. How do the children in the class experience the world? Their classroom mirrors the larger society with its diverse ethnic, religious, and socioeconomic backgrounds. Are the children learning structures for accepting and appreciating diversity at this critical age in the development of lifelong attitudes? Mere contact with diversity, without understanding, can intensify conflict. Does their classroom mirror the larger society in this sense also?

In classroom, day-care center, home, and neighborhood, kindergartners encounter rules and laws. Do they understand the reasons for these institutions? Can they distinguish between legitimate authority and raw power? Are they learning to act as rule makers as well as rule obeyers and to see the necessity of personal involvement in the democratic process?

The kindergarten class of 1988 will graduate in the year 2001 as citizens who live in a world characterized by a staggering volume of information, varying sets of values, and a growing interdependence among nations. However, children will not automatically become citizens when they graduate or reach voting age; they are citizens now, with rights, responsibilities, and a confusing array of choices before them. The abilities for making personally and socially productive decisions do not just happen. They require that the knowledge, skills, and attitudes of social studies be introduced early and built upon throughout the school years.

II. What should be the definition of and rationale for social studies for early childhood/elementary children?

The social studies are the study of political, economic, cultural, and environmental aspects of societies in the past, present, and future. For elementary school children, as well as for all age groups social studies have several purposes. The social studies equip them with the knowledge and understanding of the past necessary for coping with the present and planning for the future, enable them to understand and participate effectively in their world, and explain their relationship to other people and to social, economic, and political institutions. Social studies can provide students with the skills for productive problem solving and decision making, as well as for assessing issues and making thoughtful value judgments. Above all, the social studies help students to integrate these skills and understandings into a framework for responsible citizen participation, whether in their play group, the school, the community, or the world.

The energy, curiosity, and imagination of young children lead them to action and interaction within their environment from a narrow, unilateral perspective. They live in a family, play in a peer group, and make decisions about how they will relate to other people, what to do in their free time, with whom to play, what books to read, and how to spend money. The larger social world penetrates their lives through television and other media, travel, family, and friends; but young children lack the conceptual base to integrate the new knowledge these experiences bring. They also lack the skills to account for other perspectives in solving problems or to anticipate long-range consequences when making decisions.

A planned K-12 social studies program directs and focuses these natural characteristics to help children understand and function in their personal and social worlds. These learnings must be developed systematically from an early age, so that children move from egocentric, random observations and experiences to a broader and more structured conceptual organization. Many times, teachers suggest that at the primary level everything they do is related to social studies, but it is important to recognize that an effective social studies program cannot be just a haphazard collection of unrelated activities. It must be organized systematically around concepts from history and the social sciences.

Active, curious children need, want, and are able to learn skills that are taught and reinforced in social studies classes. These skills are required for processing information so that they can make generalizations and integrate new information into a developing system of knowledge.

Children formulate many of their attitudes and values toward society in the early years. The development of these attitudes and values occurs primarily outside the school setting. However, the social studies program should provide a setting for children to acquire knowledge of history and the social sciences and to be exposed to a broad variety of opinions, facilitating the formulation, reassessment, and affirmation of their beliefs.

The social studies program enables children to participate effectively now in the groups to which they belong and not to look only to their future participation as adults. The school itself serves as a laboratory for students to learn social participation directly and not symbolically. Democratic and participatory school and classroom environments are essential to this type of real-world learning.

If the social studies are not part of the elementary curriculum, we cannot expect our children to be prepared to understand or participate effectively in an increasingly complex world. They need to encounter and reencounter, in a variety of contexts, the knowledge, concepts, skills, and attitudes that form the foundation for participation in a democratic society. Otherwise, we are in danger of disrupting the critical balance between individual and community needs. Social studies are intended to help children understand, evaluate, and make decisions regarding these often competing claims. The problem lies in developing a learning environment and pedagogy that are intellectually and developmentally appropriate.

III. What are the goals for early childhood/elementary social studies that no other subject in the elementary curriculum can achieve?

It is understood that teaching social studies in the elementary schools is an essential part of the framework of an overall K-12 social studies program. The elementary school years are important in that they are the ones in which children develop a foundation for the entire social studies program and a beginning sense of efficacy as participating citizens of their world.

Basic skills of reading, writing, and computing are necessary but not sufficient to participate or even survive in a world demanding independent and cooperative problem solving to address complex social, economic, ethical, and personal concerns. Knowledge, skills, and attitudes necessary for informed and thoughtful participation in society require a systematically developed program focusing on concepts from history and the social sciences.

Knowledge. Social studies provide a sense of history, a sense of existence in the past as well as the present, a feeling of being in history. Even though young children find the concept of time difficult, they need to understand how the present has come about and to develop an appreciation for the heritage of this country. Huck and Kuhn (1968) state that even though children have difficulty with time concepts, they can develop an appreciation for their historical heritage through factual presentation of history, biographies of famous people, and historical fiction.

Geographic concepts are equally difficult, but the social studies provide continuing opportunities for children to understand the spatial relationships of their immediate environment as well as those of areas of the world. Scholars found that children need systematic instruction to develop map and globe skills (Rice and Cobb 1978; Crabtree 1968, 1974; Savage and Bacon 1969; Cox 1977). Children need to develop an understanding of and an appreciation for their physical and cultural environments and to consider how resources will be allocated in the future.

Concepts from anthropology and sociology provide knowledge and understanding of how the multiplicity of cultures within society and the world has developed. Children need to recognize the contributions of each culture and to explore its value system. Acquisition of concepts about racial and ethnic groups is complex, but early, planned, and structured activities can result in positive attitudes in children (Katz 1976, 234).

Knowledge from sociology, economics, and political science allows children to understand the institutions within the society and to learn about their roles within groups.

Although children easily learn concepts from economics such as work, exchange, production, and consumption, they need useful and powerful economic knowledge and the formal development of critical-thinking skills. Economic content in the early years should relate to events in children's lives as they examine buying, selling, and trading transactions, the process of making goods and services, and the origin of materials and products in their everyday lives (Armento 1986).

Skills. The skills that are primary to social studies are those related to maps and globes, such as understanding and using locational and directional terms. However, other skills that enhance students' abilities to learn, to make decisions, and to develop as competent, self-directed citizens are more meaningful and useful when developed within the context of social studies. Skills that are shared with other parts of the curriculum but may be most powerfully taught through social studies include communication skills such as writing and speaking; research skills such as collecting, organizing, and interpreting data; thinking skills such as hypothesizing, comparing, drawing inferences; decision-making skills such as considering alternatives and consequences; interpersonal skills such as seeing others' points of view, accepting responsibility, and dealing with conflict; and reading skills such as reading pictures, books, maps, charts, and graphs.

For children to develop citizenship skills appropriate to democracy, they must be capable of thinking critically about complex societal problems and global problems. Teachers must arrange the classroom environment to promote data gathering, discussion, and critical reasoning by students. Another important aspect of citizenship is that of decision maker. Children must acquire the skills of decision making, but also study the process that occurs as groups make decisions. Continually accelerating technology has created and will continue to create rapid changes in society. Children need to be equipped with the skills to cope with change.

Attitudes. The early years are ideal for children to begin to understand democratic norms and values (justice, equality, etc.)—especially in terms of the smaller social entities of the family, classroom, and community. Applying these concepts to the nation and the world is easier if one understands and appreciates them on smaller but manageable scales.

Although not uniquely in social studies, children can achieve a positive self-concept within the context of understanding the similarities and differences of people. Children need to understand that they are unique in themselves but share many similar feelings and concerns with other children. They need to understand how as individuals they can contribute to society.

Children can also develop, within the context of social studies, positive attitudes toward knowledge and learning and develop a spirit of inquiry that will enhance their understanding of their world so that they will become rational, humane, participating, effective members of a democratic society.

IV. What are the developmental characteristics of children that should be considered in planning a social studies program?

First, we need to consider that children of all ages come to school from different socioeconomic and cultural backgrounds. They come with different value systems, experiences, and learning styles, and with different feelings about themselves and the people around them. As we discuss the general characteristics of children, we recognize these individual differences.

A report from the National Association for the Education of Young Children (NAEYC) provides a helpful summary of the significant literature on the development characteristics of children.

Most five-year-olds can begin to combine simple ideas into more complex relations. They have a growing memory capacity and fine motor physical skills. They have a growing interest in the functional aspects of written language, such as recognizing meaningful words and trying to write their names (NAEYC 1986). They need an environment rich in printed materials that stimulates the development of language and literacy skills in a meaningful context. They also need a variety of direct experiences to develop cognitively, physically, emotionally, and socially. Since five-year-olds come to school with an interest in the community and the world outside their own, curriculum can expand beyond the child's immediate experience of self, home, and family (NAEYC 1986).

Six-year-olds are active learners and demonstrate considerable verbal ability. They are interested in games and rules and develop concepts and problem-solving skills from these experiences. Hands-on activity and experimentation are necessary for this age group (NAEYC 1986). Seven-year-olds become increasingly able to reason, listen to others, and show social give-and-take. Spatial relationships and time concepts are difficult for them to perceive. Flexibility, open-mindedness, and tolerance of unfamiliar ideas essential in social studies are formed to a remarkable extent by the interactions of the four- to eight-year-olds (Joyce 1970). Eight-year-olds combine great curiosity with increased social interest. They are able to learn about people who live elsewhere in the world. During these early grades, children can learn from the symbolic experiences of reading books and listening to stories; however, their understanding of what they read is based on their ability to relate the written word to their own experience (NAEYC 1986).

Research indicates that by age nine or ten children have well-established racial and ethnic prejudices and these are highly resistant to change (Joyce 1970); therefore, teachers must go beyond studies of other cultures and celebrations of their holidays and include studies of families, music, shelter, customs, beliefs, and other aspects common to all cultures (NAEYC 1986).

Nine-year-olds may be somewhat self-conscious and prefer group activities to working alone. They are beginning to understand abstractions as well as cause-and-effect relationships. Most are operating at a concrete level but need real experiences of society and social institutions such as those provided in social studies. Ten-year-olds may be experiencing bodily changes and rapid growth spurts. These changes cause periods of frustration and anger. Generally, ten-year-olds are interested in and enthusiastic about places and problems in the news. They want to know what events caused these problems, where they occurred, and the reasons for them. Most of the skills for learning social studies have been introduced by this time and they are able to apply them to new situations.

Eleven-year-olds are generally in a period of transition between childhood and adolescence. More decision making is required of them. They tend to be sociable and need opportunities to express feelings and opinions. The developmental research suggests that children at this age do not have the ability to view issues from the perspective of a whole society (Selman 1975), but need to be confronted with the types of analytical questions about history, society, and social and political behavior so important in social studies learning. Political attitudes develop very early and undergo major changes during the elementary school years. Attitudes developed by the end of elementary school are away from a personalized, benevolent government toward a more abstract, realistic idea (Greenstein 1969). The social studies also inform attitudes with accurate information from the humanities and the social sciences.

As we consider these characteristics, it becomes obvious that social studies must be an essential part of the elementary curriculum to provide the essential elements for continuing the democratic way of life. There may not be a more urgent need in the elementary school.

V. What is the research base for elementary school social studies?

What guidance does research offer in the selection of content and learning experiences for social studies to enable children to achieve the goals previously described—especially for children who will be citizens of the 21st century? Frequently, curricular patterns are not grounded either in research or in an understanding of how children learn. In fact, the social studies are often left out of the curriculum at the primary level since some educators fail to see sufficient evidence to support their inclusion (Goodlad 1984; Clegg 1977). Yet we cannot dispute the importance of an educated citizenry in maintaining, preserving, and refining a democratic society, and research points out the critical nature of early and varied learning in elementary social studies (cf. Rice 1966; Hess and Torney 1967; Atwood 1986).

Social studies concepts, based as they are in human interactions, are complex. As a result of these complexities, some would suggest that young children not be introduced to the concepts until they are mature enough to understand them. After a decade of research on early learning in social studies, Rice (1966, 3) concluded that children could learn more difficult and abstract social studies concepts much earlier than is expected in the traditional social studies curriculum. What is equally important, however, is not so much that children are capable of earlier and more complex learning, but that, if the early learning does not occur, the optimum teaching time for some concepts may pass, making it much more difficult for students to entertain new ideas or to think critically about old ones. There seem to be crucial years for certain concepts—times when students are most receptive or have developed a tolerance for or interest in emotionally powerful topics long before these topics are introduced in the curriculum. What, then, does research indicate about the process of learning particular social studies concepts?

Research findings related to the previously described goals—the development of concepts related to social studies content, the development of civic understanding, and the development of a social perspective that enables children to function at all levels of community to which they belong—highlight the significance of elementary social studies. This is not intended as an exhaustive review of the research but rather to emphasize certain studies. More comprehensive reviews can be found in William B. Stanley's *Review of Research in Social Studies Education 1976-1983* (1985), Virginia A. Atwood's *Elementary School Social Studies: Research as a Guide to Practice* (1986), and Linda Rosenzweig's *Developmental Perspective on the Social Studies* (1983). Social studies also benefit from a wide range of research in other disciplines, notably those of psycho- and sociolinguistic studies considering linkages between language and conceptual development (cf. Nelms 1987), work in cooperative learning (cf. Slavin, in press; Slavin 1981), and research in social science disciplines that inform social studies.

Time and space. History and geography, keystones of elementary as well as secondary social studies, are linked to conceptions of time and space. Yet these concepts are difficult even for some adults. Some scholars have argued, in fact, that Western society makes it especially difficult to develop a sense of time as it relates to history because Western society does not provide clear and present needs for such concepts (Poster 1973). Others have noted the culture boundedness of time conceptions, including Western, linear concepts of time. In any case, both time and space are abstract concepts formulated on relationships that are equally abstract and certainly provide difficulties for young children. This acknowledgment of the difficulty of acquiring sophisticated time and space concepts has led to some reluctance to

introduce historical and geographical content in the elementary curriculum. Recent research indicates that this reluctance may be unfounded.
- Young children who are active participants in a highly structured and sequential series of geographic inquiries can learn complex analytic processes and concepts of geography (Crabtree 1974; GENIP Committee on K-6 Geography 1987; Muessig 1987).
- Evidence indicates that children do possess complex spatial information and can abstract information from map symbols (Hewes 1982; Hatcher 1983; Park and James 1983; Liben, Moore, and Golbeck 1982).
- Children can learn cardinal directions as early as kindergarten (Lanegran, Snowfield, and Laurent 1970).
- The type of discourse used in history teaching appears to influence student interest. Children who encountered historical data in the form of biography and historical fiction exhibited interest in and enthusiasm for history and for further investigation in more traditional sources (Levstik 1986).
- Historical and geographical understanding may not be linked to the developmental patterns associated with acquiring physical time concepts (Kennedy 1983).

Economic understanding. Armento (1986) indicates that "part of the role of social studies during elementary school years is to use children's informal learning as a basis for formal development of critical-thinking skills and for the construction of useful and powerful economic knowledge."
- By age seven, children have formulated fairly accurate conceptions of work, wants, and scarcity and evidence the capability of developing a method for making decisions (Armento 1986).
- Pictures and other concretizing tools can greatly benefit children with learning disabilities and those who have not enjoyed a broad variety of experience (Armento 1986).

Social perspective. The focus on relationships between people and their environments in elementary social studies is derived from the assumption that young children need to understand both their own uniqueness and their relationship to the world. Social knowledge is constructed as students attempt to build coherent systems for thinking about and explaining their immediate environment and the elements that make up the larger world environment (Turiel 1983). Their social judgments are not random responses; rather, they are the result of the application of analysis and reason in the social world and are influenced by such factors as peer groups, adults, social and educational environments, experiences, and the institutions to which they are exposed. Social judgments also involve more than the child's "getting along" in the home or school environment. They involve the child's ability to make decisions about such issues as race and ethnicity, citizen concerns of law and justice, and social welfare and economics, many of which make competing claims in a rapidly changing world. Research on how children acquire these understandings indicates that
- Children are more open to diversity in the early elementary years than in later years (Stone 1986). A fourth grader, for instance, is more likely to express interest in studying and visiting foreign countries than an eighth grader.
- Positive self-concepts, important in positively perceiving and judging social interactions, also form during these crucial early years (Stanley 1985, 77). Particular classroom environments seem to influence the ways children develop these interactions. Teachers who appear to enjoy teaching, who include student-to-student interaction, shared decision making, and positive student-to-teacher interactions, foster more positive self-concepts in their pupils.

- Interest in and analysis of racial and ethnic differences begin early. Between the ages of six and nine, children begin to identify their own racial group as "better than the out-group" (Semaj 1980, 76).
- Acquisition of concepts about racial and ethnic groups is complex, but there is evidence that early, planned, and structured activities can result in improving positive attitudes in children (Katz 1976, 234).
- Elementary age children are already well aware of societal attitudes toward different groups (e.g., housing patterns, dating, and marriage mores). Research also indicates that elementary children can think critically about these patterns where they have sufficient experience and active involvement in discussion and inquiry (Ragan and McAulay 1973).

Civic Understanding. Research indicates that children are ready to deal with and already have ideas about civic understanding.

- As early as kindergarten, students engage in citizenship education, both covert and overt (Edwards 1986).
- Political feelings, evaluations, and attachments form well before the child learns the relevant supporting information (Greenstein 1969, 72).
- By eighth grade, children have already acquired basic orientations, and political socialization is generally well advanced by the end of elementary school (Hess and Torney 1967, 220).
- By the eighth grade, children have developed a sense of the need for consensus and majority rule in the democratic process. They have not recognized the role of debate, disagreement, and conflict in the operation of a democratic political system (Hess and Torney 1967, 216).
- A developed sense of justice and law appears to be requisite to democratic citizenship (Kohlberg 1976, 213). Particular types of classroom environments, including discussions in which students must actively think and communicate about another's reasoning, appear to facilitate this type of growth (Berkowitz 1981; Berkowitz and Gibbs 1983).

Needed research. There is much that research has not told us about teaching and learning social studies. We lack a sufficient body of basic research in many fields including research on teaching methodologies most appropriate for teaching specific social studies concepts, skills, and attitudes. We need studies of the effects of particular approaches to organizing social studies content—for instance, thematic versus chronological. These studies must take into account how children learn, another problem in need of investigation. There is also a need for further research on social studies and the exceptional child, both in terms of the exceptional child as learner and in helping other children understand and interact with exceptional children. Little has been done to investigate appropriate content and methodology for preschool and kindergarten social studies, although Carolyn Edwards' book, *Promoting Social and Moral Development in Young Children* (1986), is a thought-provoking start in that direction.

One of the most important conclusions one can draw from the available research on early learning in social studies is the critical importance of the elementary years in laying the foundation for later and increasingly mature understanding. There is reason to believe that teachers who miss these crucial opportunities to build interest, to introduce concepts from history and the social sciences, and to develop social perspectives and civic understanding may make it more difficult for citizens of the 21st century to cope with their future.

VI. What is the current status of social studies in the elementary school?

In schools throughout the United States, there are exciting classrooms where teachers challenge students to acquire the knowledge and skills necessary for making reasoned social commitments and decisions; where students hold mock trials and legislative debates to gain experience with the judicial process and the rules of debate; where they write classroom constitutions and hold elections to understand the role of the citizen in shaping political decisions; where they debate such social issues as welfare and social programs to develop an awareness of those in need of such programs; where they graph rainfall and temperatures around the country and can interpret the geographical patterns that result; where they develop travel brochures to interest students from other countries to visit their country; where they use milk cartons to build a city and can explain why certain land uses develop in areas of the city; where they hold a global olympics day to build an interest in international knowledge; or where someone role-plays a historical figure and holds a press conference for furthering knowledge of the humanity and motivations of these important persons. The overall status of social studies in elementary schools still needs improvement. We find teachers who feel unqualified to teach the content of social studies or who misinterpret them, confining instruction to a narrow focus on socialization skills or mere recall of facts from history, geography, and civics. We find that the time available for teaching the basic tools and concepts of the social sciences that can contribute to understanding human behavior receives an ever-shrinking slice of the school day. At best, this can provide only superficial treatment of this important learning. Student apathy—and even dislike—for a subject considered to be lifeless and useless is understandable in classrooms where strategies encouraging active involvement in grappling with human issues are absent; where forced marches through textbooks are frequent; and where the assumption prevails that memorization of names, places, and dates will somehow translate itself during adulthood into civic involvement. This type of curriculum does not prepare students for a future characterized by rapid change, increasing diversity, and global interdependence.

Elementary school social studies, especially in the primary grades, continue to suffer a decline in emphasis (Goodlad 1984; Cross 1977; Hahn 1985). Average instructional time ranges from approximately twenty minutes per day at the primary level to thirty-four minutes in the upper elementary grades (Lengel and Superka 1982). Some schools report very little or no social studies instruction at all in grades K-3 (Atwood 1986). This low priority is coupled with the belief of many elementary teachers that, although they are well qualified to teach reading and mathematics, they are less prepared to teach social studies (Eslinger and Superka 1982). Students themselves often characterize social studies as difficult, uninteresting, and largely irrelevant to their present and future lives. This comes as no surprise in light of reports that the dominant classroom pattern is characterized by lecture and recitation, reading textbooks, and completing worksheets. Goodlad's 1984 study confirms earlier reports that, even when students express a high interest in social studies topics, classroom treatment tends to reduce these topics to recitation of dates and places and displaces opportunities to explore relationships, draw inferences about human behavior, and make in-depth cultural comparisons.

Goodlad found that at the primary level the social studies curriculum is blurred by lack of common agreement about what is to be taught. A predominant theme appears to be an effort to help students understand themselves and others in the context of family and community. These topics are punctuated by occasional—and often superficial—attention to other cultures.

At the upper elementary level, history, geography, and civics become solidly established in the curriculum. The major emphasis is on the United States with additional time allocated to world history and geography. However, pressure increases to memorize more and more low-level information (Atwood 1986). Although teachers list thinking and decision-making skills prominently among goals for students, actual practice reveals vastly different priorities. Essay tests are rare, and opportunities to engage in the problem-solving and inquiry activities that are key ingredients in citizen efficacy are notably absent from most classrooms. The prevailing inattention to international topics and in-depth cultural comparisons leaves little mystery as to why more than 50 percent of the students in Goodlad's study perceived other countries and their ideologies as threatening to the United States. He concludes that many elementary teachers have not identified the curricular components necessary for understanding the United States in a global context. Relying solely on reading textbooks, completing worksheets, taking tests, and listening eliminates the active, participatory power of social studies that is essential to the education of citizens in a democracy.

Newmann (1986) notes that a trend toward minimal civic participation among adults can be expected to continue. Most people's only foray into the public arena is voting or temporary involvement in single-issue politics. Strikingly absent is a feeling of personal trusteeship of general civic welfare. The current agenda of most schools lack the components for converting into reality the stated goal of producing active, informed citizens. In a complex, interdependent world, students remain ethnocentric. In a participatory political culture, they receive scant opportunity to learn participation. In an era of rapidly expanding knowledge, they have few chances to develop the structures necessary for sifting and evaluating the vast amount of information constantly streaming at them through the media.

VII. How should we prepare teachers of early childhood and elementary social studies?

Effective early childhood/elementary social studies as described earlier in this paper will not just happen. If the status of early childhood/elementary social studies education is to change, then the education of teachers who have the responsibility for teaching those children will be a critical factor. Teacher education in social studies has the task of educating teachers with sufficient content knowledge in history and the social sciences; knowledge about and skill in different teaching techniques; an ability to locate, evaluate, and use appropriate resources to supplement the text; sufficient knowledge regarding the characteristics and abilities of young children; and an enthusiasm for teaching social studies that comes from an understanding of the importance of social studies in the early years and an appreciation for and understanding of social studies content.

NCSS has adopted Standards for the Preparation of Social Studies Teachers (1988) to address these goals. It leaves to the individual states and teacher education institutions to design specific programs around these standards. The NCSS standards specify that "candidates for initial licensure as social studies teachers should have gained substantial understanding of the information, concepts, theories, analytical approaches and differing values perspectives, including global and multicultural perspectives, important to teaching social studies. Problem-solving, critical-thinking, and application skills should be stressed." The standards recognize, however, that teaching social studies to children requires more. The standards further state that "courses in social studies methods should prepare prospective teachers to select, integrate, and translate knowledge and methodology from history and social science disciplines in ways appropriate to students in the school level they will teach and give attention to the goals unique to the social studies and those shared jointly with other areas of the school curriculum. Students should also be able to teach social studies utilizing a variety of curriculum approaches and in different types of settings."

Early childhood and elementary school teachers must be well versed in learning and motivation theories. They need to understand cognitive and psychosocial development and its relationship to the teaching and learning processes. They need to be able to integrate concepts, processes, and examples from science, literature, mathematics, music, art, and social studies. They must understand the effects of sociopolitical and economic variables on families and, consequently, on children. It is critical for prospective teachers to observe and work with children in order for them to assimilate, synthesize, and substantiate all that is learned in a program.

The goals of social studies dictate that elementary school teachers have certain experiences, skills, values, and knowledge. Multicultural experiences for prospective elementary teachers are crucial. Studies have shown that the numbers of minority children in schools are growing while the numbers of minority teachers are declining; these phenomena affect elementary social studies in two ways. Teachers need to be well grounded in multicultural education so that they can teach about it, and they need to be sensitive to the needs of minority children. Jantz and Klawiller (1985, 82) state that attitudes about race crystallize during the later elementary years and "the attitudes expressed by teachers and peers are important in the elaboration of racial attitudes."

VIII. What type of continued professional development is needed for early childhood/elementary social studies teachers?

Teaching must be seen as continuous learning. Initial certification only commences the process. Continued professional development should be shaped and controlled by the continuously evolving research related to teaching methodologies, child development, learning principles, and new technological developments that may be used in instruction. Teachers must remain knowledgeable of changing demographic patterns of the nation and accompanying changes in student characteristics. New knowledge in history and the social sciences, current issues, controversial issues, and evolving social conditions requires the constant attention of the teacher.

Programs of individual professional growth may include such experiences as attendance and participation in conventions, in-service courses and workshops, travel and exchange programs, postgraduate studies, participation in professional organizations, reading of desirable professional literature, and self-evaluations (Dobkin, Fischer, Ludwig, and Kobliner 1985).

Professional development within the local school district should provide: (1) a well-organized teacher development and evaluation program; (2) support staff for instructional improvement; (3) appropriate social studies materials and resources; (4) a functioning social studies curriculum committee; (5) a K-12, systemwide, articulated social studies program that is regularly reviewed and updated; (6) opportunities for teachers to participate in professional social studies organizations at a local, state, and national level; and (7) a professional library that contains social studies periodicals, research studies, social studies texts, and related literature.

State and national professional organizations should be involved in the professional growth activities of teachers. Of the many contributions these professional organizations make, the publication of significant literature is one of the most important. These organizations should also act as a voice for improving education in general.

Professional growth programs will influence and control teachers' abilities throughout their professional careers. It is imperative that each individual make a personal commitment to professional growth and through that commitment provide effective and exciting social studies for early childhood/ elementary children.

IX. Appropriate number of daily minutes for social studies teaching in the elementary school

Given the importance of social studies in the elementary school, NCSS recommends that 20 percent of the academic day which includes reading/language arts, science, mathematics, and the arts, be devoted to social studies instruction.

X. Summary

If the young people of this nation are to become effective participants in a democratic society, then social studies must be an essential part of the curriculum in the early childhood/ elementary years. In a world that demands independent and cooperative problem solving to address complex social, economic, ethical, and personal concerns, the social studies are as basic for survival as reading, writing, and computing. Knowledge, skills, and attitudes necessary for informed and thoughtful participation in society require a systematically developed program focused on concepts from history and the social sciences.

References

Armento, B. J. "Research on Teaching Social Studies." In *Handbook of Research on Teaching*, 3d ed. Edited by M.C. Wittrock. New York: Macmillan, 1986.

Association of American Colleges. "Integrity in the College Curriculum: A Report to the Academic Community." *Chronicle of Higher Education* 29, no. 22 (1985): 12 -30.

Atwood, V. A., ed. *Elementary Social Studies: Research as a Guide to Practice*. Washington, D.C.: National Council for the Social Studies, 1986.

Berkowitz, M. W. "A Critical Appraisal of the Educational and Psychological Perspectives on Moral Discussion." *Journal of Educational Thought* 15. 1981: 20-33.

Berkowitz, M. W, and J. C. Gibbs. "Measuring the Developmental Feature of a Moral Discussions." *Merrill-Palmer Quarterly* 29. 1983: 339-440,

Carnegie Corporation Task Force on Teaching as Profession. *A Nation Prepared. Teachers for the Twenty-first Century*. New York: Carnegie Forum on Education and the Economy, Carnegie Corporation of New York, 1986.

Carnegie Foundation for the Advancement of Teaching. "College: The Undergraduate Experience in America." *Chronicle of Higher Education* 33, no. 10 (1986): 16-22.

Clegg, A. "Three Midwest Cities: The Status of Social Studies Education." *Social Education* 41, no. 7 (1977): 585-87.

Cox, W. "Children's Map-reading Abilities with Large-scale Urban Maps." Doctoral dissertation. Madison: University of Wisconsin, 1977.

Crabtree, C. *Teaching Geography in Grades One through Three. Effects of Instruction in the Core Concept of Geographic Theory* (Project No. 5-1037). Washington: Department of Health, Education, and Welfare, Office of Education, 1968.

_____. *Children's Thinking Skills in the Social Studies*, Part 1: *Some Factors of Sequence and Transfer in Learning Skills of Geographic Analysis*. Los Angeles: University of California, 1974.

Dobkin, S. W., J. Fischer, B. Ludwig, and R. Kobliner, eds. A *Handbook for the Teaching of Social Studies*, 2d ed. Newton, Mass.: Allyn and Bacon, Inc., 1985.

Downey, M. "Teaching the History of Childhood." *Social Education* 50. 1986: 262-67.

Edwards, C. P. *Promoting Social and Moral Development in Young Children*. New York: Teachers College, Columbia, 1986.

Eslinger, M. V, and D. P. Superka. "Teachers." In *Social Studies in the 1980s: A Report of Project SPAN*, Edited by Irving Morrissett. Alexandria, Va.: Association for Supervision and Curriculum Development, 1982.

Freeman, E., and L. Levstik. "Recreating the Past: Historical Fiction in the Social Studies Curriculum. *Elementary School Journal* 88, no. 14 (1988): 329-37

Gander, M. J., and H W Garoiller. *Child and Adolescent Development*. Boston: Little, Brown and Co., 1981.

Geographic Education National Implementation Project (GENIP) Committee on K-6 Geography. *K-6 Geography: Themes, Key Ideas, and Learning Opportunities*. Washington, D.C.: Geographic Education National Implementation Project, 1987.

Goodlad, J. I. *A Place Called School.* New York: McGraw-Hill, 1984.
Greenstein, F. l. *Children and Politics.* New Haven, Conn.: Yale University Press, 1969.
Gross, R. E. "The Status of the Social Studies in the Public Schools of the United States: Fact and Impressions of a National Survey." *Social Education* 41, 1977.
Hahn, C. L. "The Status of the Social Studies in the Public Schools of the United States: Another Look." *Social Education* 49, no. 3, 1985.
Hatcher, B. "Putting Young Cartographers 'On the Map.'" *Childhood Education* 59 (1983): 311-15.
Hess, R. D., and J.V Torney. *The Development of Political Attitudes in Children.* Chicago: Aldine, 1967.
Hewes, D. W. "Preschool Geography: Developing a Sense of Self in Time and Space." *Journal of Geography* 81 (1982): 94-97.
Holmes Group. *Tomorrow's Teachers.* East Lansing, Mich.: Holmes Group, Inc., 1986.
Huck, Charlotte S., and Doris Young Kuhn. *Children's Literature in the Elementary School.* New York: Holt, Rinehart and Winston, 1968.
Jantz, R. K., and K. Klawiller. "Early Childhood/Elementary Social Studies: A Review of Recent Research." *Review of Research in Social Studies Education 1976-1983.* Edited by W.B. Stanley. Washington, D.C.: National Council for the Social Studies, 1985.
Joyce, B. R. "Social Action for Primary Schools." *Childhood Education* 46, no. 5, 1970.
Katz, P. A. *Toward the Elimination of Racism.* New York: Pergamon Press, 1976.
Kennedy, K. J. "Assessing the Relationship between Information Processing Capacity and Historical Understanding." *Theory and Research in Social Education* 11, no. 2 (1983): 1-22.
Kohlberg, L. "This Special Section in Perspective." *Social Education* 40 (1976): 213-15.
Lanegran, D. A., J. G. Snowfield, and A. Lavent. "Retarded Children and the Concepts of Distance and Direction." *Journal of Geography* 69 (1970): 157-60.
Lengel, J. G., and D. P. Superka. "Curriculum Patterns." In *Social Studies in the 1980s. A Report of Project SPAN.* Edited by Irving Morrissett. Alexandria, Va.: Association for Supervision and Curriculum Development, 1982.
Levstik, L. "The Relationship between Historical Response and Narrative in a Sixth Grade Classroom." *Theory and Research in Social Education* 41, no. 1 (1986): 1-15.
Levstik, L., and C. Pappas. "Exploring the Development of Historical Understanding." *Journal of Research and Development in Education* 21, no. 1 (1987): 1-15.
Liben, L. S., M. L. Moore, and S. L. Golbeck. "Preschooler's Knowledge of Their Classroom Environment: Evidence from Small-scale and Life-size Spatial Task." *Childhood Development.* 53 (1982): 1275-84.
Muessig, R. "An Analysis of Developments in Geographic Education." The *Elementary School Journal* 87, no. 5 (1987): 571-89.
NAEYC. "Position Statement on Developmentally Appropriate Practice in Early Childhood Programs Serving Children from Birth through Age 8." *Young Children* (September 1986): 4-19.
NCSS. "Standards for the Preparation of Social Studies Teachers." *Social Education* 52 (1988): 10-12.
Nelms, B. F. "Response and Responsibility: Reading, Writing, and Social Studies." *Elementary School Journal* 87, no. 5 (1987): 571-89.
Newmann, F. M. "Priorities for the Future: Toward a Common Agenda." *Social Education* 50, no. 4, 1986.
Park, D. C., and C. Q. James. "Effect of Encoding Instructions on Children's Spatial and Color Memory: Is There Evidence of Automaticity?" *Child Development* 54 (1983): 61-68.
Poster, J. B. "The Birth of the Past: Children's Perception of Historical Time." *History Teacher* (1973): 581-98.
Ragan, W., and J. McAulay. *Social Studies for Today's Children,* 2d ed. New York: Appleton-Century-Crofts, 1973.
Rice, M. J. *Educational Stimulation in the Social Studies: Analysis and Interpretation of Research.* Athens: Research and Development Center in Education Stimulation, University of Georgia, 1966.
Rice, M. J., and R. L. Cobb. *What Can Children Learn in Geography? A Review of the Research.* Boulder: SSEC, 1978.
Rosenzweig, L. *Developmental Perspectives on the Social Studies,* Bulletin 66. Washington, D.C.: National Council for the Social Studies, 1983.
Savage, T. S., Jr., and P. Bacon. "Teaching Symbolic Map Skills with Primary Grade Children." *Journal of Geography* 68 (1969): 326-32.
Selman, R. L. "A Developmental Approach to Interpersonal and Moral Awareness in Young Children: Some Theoretical and Educational Implications of Levels of Social Perspective Taking. In *Values Education.* Edited by J. Meyer, B. Barnham, and J. Cholvat. Waterloo, Ontario: Wilfrid Laurier University Press, 1975: 233-49.
Semaj, L. "The Development of Racial Evaluation and Preference: A Cognitive Approach." *Journal of Black Psychology* 6 (1980): 59-79.
Slavin, R.E. "Synthesis of Research on Cooperative Learning." *Educational Leadership* 38, no. 8 (1981): 655-59.
_____. "Cooperative Learning: Where Behavioral and Humanistic Approaches to Classroom Motivation Meet." *Elementary School Journal.* In press.

Stanley, W. B. *Review of Research in Social Studies Education: 1976-1983.* Washington, D.C.: National Council for the Social Studies, 1985.

Stone, L.C. "International and Multicultural Education." In *Elementary Social Studies: Research as a Guide to Practice.* Edited by V. Atwood. Washington, D.C.: National Council for the Social Studies, 1986.

Thornton, S., and R. Vukelich. "Effects of Children's Understanding of Time Concepts on Historical Understanding." *Theory and Research in Social Education*, 1988: 69-82.

Turiel, E. *The Development of Social Knowledge: Morality and Convention.* New Rochelle: Cambridge University Press, 1983.

VanderZanden, J. W. *Human Development.* New York: Alfred A. Knopf, 1985.

* Task Force

"Nucleus Committee"
Dorothy J. Skeel, Chair, Peabody College of Vanderbilt, Nashville, Tennessee
Virginia A. Atwood, University of Kentucky, Lexington, Kentucky
Buckley Barnes, Georgia State University, Atlanta, Georgia
Maria Cruz, Dade County Public Schools, Miami, Florida
Edi Guyton, Georgia State University, Atlanta, Georgia
Linda Levstik, University of Kentucky, Lexington, Kentucky
Patricia Van Decar, Georgia Southern College, Statesboro, Georgia

Members
Susan Austin, Research for Better Schools, Philadelphia, Pennsylvania
Phyllis Clarke, Boulder Valley Public Schools, Boulder, Colorado
Carol Hamilton Cobb, Metropolitan Nashville Schools, Nashville, Tennessee
Lois "Frankie" Daniel, Millcreek Elementary School, Lexington, Kentucky
Francis Davis, Dougherty County Schools, Georgia
Wayne Dumas, University of Missouri, Columbia, Missouri
Judith M. Finkelstein, Price Laboratory School, Northern Iowa University, Cedar Falls, Iowa
Charles J. Fox, Kansas City Schools, Kansas City, Kansas
Michael Hartoonian, Wisconsin Department of Public Instruction, Madison, Wisconsin
Lillian G. Katz, University of Illinois, Champaign-Urbana, Illinois
Willard M. Kniep, Global Perspective in Education, Inc., New York, New York
Ellen Kronowitz, California State University, San Bernardino, California
Morris Lamb, Southern Illinois University at Carbondale
Margit McGuire, Seattle Pacific University, Seattle, Washington
Mabel McKinney-Browning, American Bar Association, Chicago, Illinois
Debra Miller, Belmont Street Community School, Worcester, Massachusetts
Charles Mitsakos, Winchester Public Schools, Winchester, Massachusetts
Raymond Muessig, Ohio State University, Columbus, Ohio
Jack Nelson, Rutgers University, New Brunswick, New Jersey
Mary Jacque Northup, Plainview Schools, Plainview, Texas
Anna S. Ochoa, Indiana University, Bloomington, Indiana
Linda W Rosenzweig, Chatham College, Pittsburgh, Pennsylvania
Huber M. Walsh, University of Missouri-St. Louis, Missouri
Myra Zarnowski, Queens College, New York, New York

Essential Characteristics of a Citizenship Education Program

Prepared by Citizenship Committee

Approved by NCSS Board of Directors 1983

POSITION STATEMENT & GUIDELINES

Citizenship education has been a central focus of schooling throughout United States history. Despite recent rhetoric that citizenship should become a *new* basic in education, social studies educators recognize the historical significance it has occupied in schooling throughout our country's history. Horace Mann, for example, more than a hundred years ago wrote:

> In order that men may be prepared for self-government, their apprenticeship must commence in childhood. The great moral attribute of self-government cannot be born and matured in a day; and if school children are not trained to it, we only prepare ourselves for disappointment.[1]

Certainly, nearly all who seek to reform or revitalize education in the U.S. today include discussion regarding citizenship education. In citing social studies among the five "new" basics, the National Commission on Excellence in Education in its report outlines a three year high school program in social studies. That report emphasizes the goal of citizenship education when it concludes, "An understanding of each of these areas is requisite to the informed and committed exercise of citizenship in our free society."[2]

The National Council for the Social Studies has long recognized the centrality of citizenship education in the social studies. The significant role of citizenship education is clearly reflected in the basic documents of the National Council for the Social Studies. The NCSS Curriculum Guidelines assert "the basic goal of social studies education is to prepare young people to be humane, rational, participating citizens in a world that is becoming increasingly interdependent."[3] Further, the NCSS position statement on the Essentials of the Social Studies says that "citizenship participation in public life is essential to the health of our democratic system. Effective social studies programs help prepare young people who can identify, understand, and work to solve the problems that face our increasingly diverse nation and interdependent world."[4]

The Essential Characteristics of a Citizenship Education Program Form (following page) was developed with specific reference to the NCSS Curriculum Guidelines. This form will assist school system personnel in better determining the effectiveness of their educational programs in the area of citizenship education.

Notes

[1] Quoted in Byron G. Massialas, *Education and the Political System*. Addison Wesley, 1969: 2.
[2] "A Nation At Risk: The Imperative for Educational Reform." Final draft of The National Commission on Excellence in Education, April 1983: 18.
[3] A Revision of the NCSS Social Studies Curriculum Guidelines, *Social Education* 43, (April 1979): 266.
[4] Statement on Essentials of Social Studies. *Social Education* 45, March 1981.

Essential Characteristics of a Citizenship Program: Criteria Checklist

Check/respond as appropriate

Model Citizenship Program	Assessment of Current Program			Model Citizenship Program	Assessment of Current Program		
	Current program does this (X)	Grade level(s) where this occurs	Evidence this occurs		Current program does this (X)	Grade level(s) where this occurs	Evidence this occurs
• Is based upon objectives that are thoughtfully selected and are philosophically consistent with the "Essentials of the Social Studies" and are clearly stated in such a way as to furnish direction for the entire program.				• Provides opportunities for investigation into public policy issues.			
• Is built on a logical developmental K-12 sequence that attempts to develop the cognitive structure, skills, attitudes, and knowledge necessary for full participation in local, state, national, and global communities.				• Enables students to practice civic participation in the total school program, including school governance, for development of skills for democratic political participation. Encourages students to participate in civic activities in the community.			
• Recognizes that while the primary responsibility for citizenship education resides with social studies educators, it is also an integral part of the total school program including school climate, procedures, and organization.				• Provides students with a broad range of educational experiences to ensure that classroom settings are culturally rich, intellectually stimulating, and experientially based.			
• Is based upon learning experiences that are meaningful and practical to students and that enable them to discuss issues in an open, supportive environment, i.e., such instruction should be directly related to the age, maturity, and concepts of students.				• Provides opportunities for students to learn about and appreciate multicultural contributions to our civic heritage.			
• Provides students with understanding and appreciation of the fundamental beliefs inherent in the Declaration of Independence, the U.S. Constitution, and the Universal Declaration of Human Rights through learning experiences that are rooted in the historical derivation as well as the contemporary application of these documents.				• Helps students see themselves as members of various structures including family, other groups, the local community, the state, and the nation, and as inhabitants of a global society.			
• Provides formal instruction for all students in concepts related to the structures and function of local, state, and national government, international organizations, and processes and judicial systems at all levels.				• Provides students with opportunities to identify their rights and responsibilities as members of various groups, e.g., family, school, community, state, nation, and the human species in a global community.			
• Focuses instruction upon study of the United States in global and historical contexts.				• Develops student competency in generating and using standards of justice, ethics, morality, and practicality to make judgments about people, institutions, policies, and decisions.*			
				• Is sensitive to parents, interested individuals, and civic groups.			
				• Includes comprehensive evaluation using a variety of measures to assess achievement of objectives.			
				• Systematically, formally evaluates to maintain and upgrade program quality.			

* Richard C. Remy, *Handbook of Basic Citizenship Competencies*. Alexandria, Va.: Association for Supervision and Curriculum Development, 1980: 86.

Global Education

Prepared by International Activities Committee

Approved by NCSS Board of Directors 1981

POSITION STATEMENT & GUIDELINES

Technological advances, increased trade, tourism and cultural exchanges, environmental concerns, competition for markets and scarce resources, and the continuing arms race are drawing nations and people into increasingly complex relationships. Increased human interactions across national and continental boundaries increase the potential for both cooperation and conflict. The day-to-day lives of average citizens, as well as the destinies of nations, are being influenced by our growing international, cross-cultural links.

The phenomenon of globalization is evident in a variety of ways, including: (1) the evolution of global systems of communication and transportation; (2) the incorporation of local, regional, and national economies into a world-wide global economy; (3) increased interaction between societies, resulting in a global culture which exists along with an array of distinctive local, national, and regional cultures; (4) the emergence of a world-wide international system which is eroding the traditional boundaries between domestic and international politics; (5) the increasing effect of human activity upon the planet's ecosystem and the increasing constraints on human activity imposed by the limits of the system; and (6) an expanding global consciousness that enhances awareness of our identities as members of the human species, as inhabitants of the planet Earth, and as participants in a global system.

Human life has been globalized to the point where we must alter the ways we have commonly viewed ourselves and others. The view of the world as a collection of countries pursuing separate destinies is no longer accurate. Rather, globalization has progressed to the point where each of us is constantly touched by interactions within the global system.

The growing interrelatedness of life on our planet has increased the need for citizens to possess the knowledge and sensitivity required to comprehend the global dimensions of political, economic, and cultural phenomena. Although highly trained specialists in foreign languages and in international affairs play a vital role in our nation's transnational interactions, it is imperative in a democracy that public understanding of global events and processes be widely shared. Our nation's security, prosperity, and way of life are dependent in large part on citizens developing the capacity to comprehend transnational, cross-cultural interactions and to participate constructively in decisions influencing foreign policy.

The Meaning of Global Education

Global education refers to efforts to cultivate in young people a perspective of the world which emphasizes the interconnections among cultures, species, and the planet. The purpose of global education is to develop in youth the knowledge, skills, and attitudes needed to live effectively in a world possessing limited natural resources and characterized by ethnic diversity, cultural pluralism, and increasing interdependence. The need to improve the international orientation of children and youth is widely recognized. Nonetheless, concerted efforts to upgrade and expand the global dimensions of elementary and secondary curricula are not widespread. Furthermore, only a small percentage of those students who attend college have transnational, cross-cultural experiences or enroll in courses in international studies. Thus, for most citizens, the elementary and secondary schools are important agencies in our society for nurturing constructive attitudes toward global matters and for providing basic knowledge about international events and processes. It is clear that the foundation for our understanding of world events, the impact of international issues on our daily lives, and the interrelatedness of peoples and of cultures must be built at the elementary and secondary levels.

The National Council for the Social Studies recognizes the urgent need to improve and to expand the global dimensions of the social studies curriculum. The recommendations offered here follow from the *NCSS Curriculum Guidelines*, which state that "the basic goal of social studies education is to prepare young people to be humane, rational, participating citizens in a world that is becoming increasingly interdependent." The framework of the *Guidelines* presents four goal areas for the social studies: knowledge, abilities, valuing, and social participation. Global education should be interpreted and implemented within this framework. A global perspective should permeate the total spectrum of social studies goals, offerings, materials, and instructional strategies. Global education needs to be viewed as part of the foundation of social studies education and as being more fundamentally important than a mere addition to the curriculum.

The subject matter and values of global education should not be limited to social studies. However, due to the type of academic and professional training that they have received and the nature of the subject matter of social studies, social studies teachers are in a key position to play a leading role in bringing a global perspective to the school curriculum at the building and district levels.

The two major thrusts of these guidelines are that social studies should assume a major role in providing students with opportunities (1) to learn to perceive and understand the world as a global system, and (2) to see themselves as participants in that system, recognizing the benefits, costs, rights, and responsibilities inherent in such participation.

Recommendations

The social studies should emphasize

- *that the human experience is an increasingly globalized phenomenon in which people are constantly being influenced by transnational, crosscultural, multi-cultural, multi-ethnic interactions.*

  Viewing human experience only in relation to a North American or a European frame of reference has been a long-standing bias in education in the United States. Today, the social studies should include a world-centered treatment of humankind. For example. the teaching of history can be improved by the use of a global approach to the study of our past and by the addition to the curriculum of more content focused on developing nations and domestic minorities.

- *the variety of actors on the world stage.*

  The dramatic increase in transnational interactions in recent years has produced growing numbers of individuals, groups, and agencies with international contacts and influence. The character and influence of multinational corporations, church groups, scientific and cultural organizations, United Nations agencies, and local, state, and federal agencies deserve fuller treatment in the social studies curriculum.

- *that humankind is an integral part of the world environment.*

  The human-natural environment should be seen as a single system. This requires an emphasis on: (1) the ultimate dependence of humankind upon natural resources; (2) the fact that natural resources are limited; (3) the nature of the planet's ecosystem; and (4) the impact of ecological laws on human culture.

- *the linkages between present social, political, and ecological realities and alternative futures.*

  Students should perceive the close relationships between past, present, and future. The use of "historical flashbacks," for example, can add to students' understanding of the

relation of past to present. Greater emphasis is needed on studies designed to improve students' ability to see present choices as links to possible alternative futures.
- *citizen participation in world affairs.*
World affairs have often been treated as a spectator sport in which only the "expert" can participate. The increasing globalization of the human condition has created additional opportunities and responsibilities for individuals and groups to take personal, social, and political action in the international arena. The curriculum should demonstrate that individuals and groups can influence and can be influenced by world events. Furthermore, the social studies curriculum should help to develop the understandings, skills, and attitudes needed to respond effectively and responsibly to world events.

The Realities of Educational Change

Sound educational responses to the challenges of interdependence, cultural diversity, and competition for scarce natural resources require careful attention to the realities of educational change. Efforts to improve global education in the schools must take into account the fact that schools are complex human organizations subject to many demands and pressures. Individuals and groups involved in our educational system include: parents, students, teachers, administrators, local curriculum committees, professional educational associations, accrediting agencies, textbook publishers, state departments of education, and special interest groups. In light of these realities, improvements in global education, like general educational reform efforts, require: (1) that a thorough assessment be made of existing opportunities to encourage global education and that obstacles to those efforts be identified and confronted; (2) that specific practical steps be taken to strengthen ongoing programs in global education; (3) that successful experimental efforts in global education be expanded; and (4) that new initiatives in global education be stimulated.

To become a more effective agent of citizen education in a global age, the schools in general and the social studies in particular need to continue to expand efforts to globalize the curriculum. The National Council for the Social Studies urges such action and offers a variety of materials and services to help social studies educators get on with this important task.

* The analysis in this section is taken largely from *Schooling and Citizenship in a Global Age* by Lee Anderson.

Study About Religions in the Social Studies Curriculum

Prepared by Religion in the Schools Committee

Approved by NCSS Board of Directors 1984

POSITION STATEMENT & GUIDELINES

The National Council for the Social Studies in its *Statement on Essentials of the Social Studies* declares that:

> Students need a knowledge of the world at large and the world at hand, the world of individuals and the world of institutions, the world past, and the world present and future.

Religions have influenced the behavior of both individuals and nations, and have inspired some of the world's most beautiful art, architecture, literature, and music. History, our own nation's religious pluralism, and contemporary world events are testimony that religion has been and continues to be an important cultural value. The NCSS Curriculum Guidelines state that "the social studies program should draw from currently valid knowledge representative of human experience, culture, and beliefs." The study about religions, then, has "a rightful place in the public school curriculum because of the pervasive nature of religious beliefs, practices. institutions, and sensitivities."

Knowledge about religions is not only a characteristic of an educated person but is also absolutely necessary for understanding and living in a world of diversity. Knowledge of religious differences and the role of religion in the contemporary world can help promote understanding and alleviate prejudice. Since the purpose of the social studies is to provide students with a knowledge of the world that has been, the world that is, and the world of the future, studying about religions should be an essential part of the social studies curriculum. Omitting study about religions gives students the impression that religions have not been and are not now part of the human experience. Study about religions may be dealt with in special courses and units or wherever and whenever knowledge of the religious dimension of human history and culture is needed for a balanced and comprehensive understanding. In its 1963 decision in the case of *Abington v. Schempp*, the United States Supreme Court declared that study about religions in the nation's public schools is both legal and desirable. Justice Tom Clark writing the majority opinion stated:

> In addition, it might well be said that one's education is not complete without a study of comparative religions or the history of religion and its relationship to the advancement of civilization. It certainly may be said that the Bible is worthy of study for its literary and historical qualities. Nothing we have said here indicates that such study of the Bible or of religion, when presented objectively as part of a secular program of education, may not be effected consistent with the first Amendment.

Justice William Brennan in a concurring opinion wrote:

> The holding of the Court today plainly does not foreclose teaching about the Holy Scriptures or about the differences between religious sects in classes in literature or history. Indeed, whether or not the Bible is involved, it would be impossible to teach meaningfully many subjects in the social sciences or the humanities without some mention of religion.

If the public schools are to provide students with a comprehensive education in the social studies, academic study about religions should be a part of the curriculum.

Guidelines

1. Study about religions should strive for awareness and understanding of the diversity of religions, religious experiences, religious expressions, and the reasons for particular expressions of religious beliefs within a society or culture.
2. Study about religions should stress the influence of religions on history, culture, the arts, and contemporary issues.
3. Study about religions should permit and encourage a comprehensive and balanced examination of the entire spectrum of ideas and attitudes pertaining to religion as a component of human culture.
4. Study about religions should investigate a broad range, both geographic and chronological, of religious beliefs, practices, and values.
5. Study about religions should examine the religious dimension of human existence in its broader cultural context, including its relation to economic, political, and social institutions as well as its relation to the arts, language, and literature.
6. Study about religions should deal with the world's religions from the same perspective (i.e., beginnings, historical development, sacred writings, beliefs, practices, values, and effect on history, culture, contemporary issues, and the arts).
7. Study about religions should be objective.
8. Study about religions should be academic in nature, stressing student awareness and understanding, not acceptance and/or conformity.
9. Study about religions should emphasize the necessity and importance of tolerance, respect, and mutual understanding in a nation and world of diversity.
10. Study about religions should be descriptive, non-confessional, and conducted in an environment free of advocacy.
11. Study about religions should seek to develop and utilize the various skills, attitudes, and abilities that are essential to history and the social sciences (i.e., locating, classifying, and interpreting data; keen observation; critical reading, listening, and thinking; questioning; and effective communication).
12. Study about religions should be academically responsible and pedagogically sound, utilizing accepted methods and materials of the social sciences, history, and literature.
13. Study about religions should involve a range of materials that provide a balanced and fair treatment of the subject, and distinguish between confessional and historical fact.
14. Study about religions should be conducted by qualified and certified teachers selected for their academic knowledge, their sensitivity and empathy for differing religious points of view, and their understanding of the Supreme Court's decisions pertaining to religious practices and study about religions in the public schools.

[1] "Statement on Essentials of the Social Studies." *Social Education* 45 (March 1981): 163.
[2] "A Revision of the NCSS Social Studies Curriculum Guidelines." *Social Education* 43 (April 1979): 268.
[3] William E. Collie and Lee H. Smith. "Teaching About Religion in the Schools: The Continuing Challenge." *Social Education* 45 (January 1981): 16.

Teaching about Science, Technology and Society in Social Studies: Education for Citizenship in the 21st Century

Prepared by the Science and Society Committee

Approved by NCSS Board of Directors 1989

Rationale

POSITION STATEMENT & GUIDELINES

Long before recorded history, technology played an important role in humans' search for improving their existence. The stone axe, the use of fire to provide heat and to prepare food, and the development of the wheel are just three results of humans' search for solutions to their problems and to continued improvements in the quality of their lives. The strong interrelationship between the desire to explain the natural environment and to improve human existence has been historically the impetus for technological developments.

Until a few hundred years ago, solutions to problems were based, for the most part, on tradition and on change that occurred slowly. Each new generation lived in a world much like that of its ancestors. The development of science, both as a way of knowing and as a body of knowledge, ushered in profound changes. As our scientific knowledge has grown so also has our ability to apply that knowledge to everyday problems. Today, we can split the atom, manufacture artificial hearts and kidneys, dissect human genes, and create mind-altering drugs and artificial intelligence. Robots aid us and our spacecraft are poised to explore the universe. The pace of change is now so rapid one can hardly predict what life will be like in the next decade let alone 100 years into the future.

In most cases, the study of our natural and built world, as well as new knowledge and technology, enriches and extends our lives. It also brings unanticipated side effects, hidden costs, and a constant demand for alternative ways of doing things. As scientific knowledge has increased and technology has become more complex and pervasive, people have found that technology can bring major benefits as well as significant costs to society.

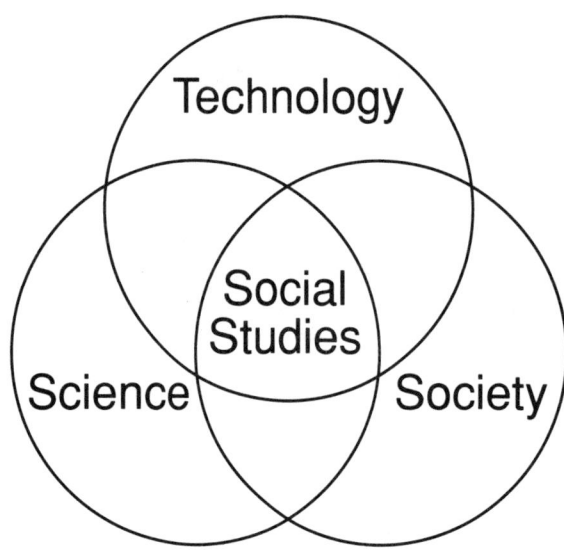

STS Education: the understanding of how science and technology shape and are shaped by society, the problems and opportunities they create, and how citizens can relate most effectively to them.

Science and technology present democratic societies with certain challenges. These challenges include finding a balance between the expectations of the freedom to inquire that spurs scientific research and inventiveness and democratic values, including the belief that the general population should directly or indirectly have a hand in making public policy. The idea that each person is entitled to a voice in determining public policy is deeply embedded in our society. As issues become increasingly complex, uninformed votes can threaten the very democratic principles that encourage scientific and technological inquiries and applications. Clearly, technology plays a role in shaping our values, but also the values of people in previous generations have also shaped the science and technology we have, just as our values will help determine the science and technology of the future. Values and beliefs regarding the quality of life in tandem with technology make such advancements as genetic engineering possible. The future of such activities lies not so much with science and technology but with the social context reflecting the values and beliefs in which they exist.

The European settlement of North America and the development of our nation have, in part, been a direct product of scientific and technological thought and knowledge. Our society and culture have shaped rapid technological advancements and have been shaped by them throughout its brief history. Currently, the distinction between social and scientific issues is not sharp. It is difficult to think of a vital social issue where a discussion and resolution of any of today's important issues does not require a meaningful consideration of concepts and skills from science, technology, and the social sciences. Exercising our civic responsibilities requires an increasing level of scientific and technological competency and a knowledge and understanding of the interdependence and interaction among science, technology, and society. If the general public is to participate actively in making public policy decisions, the level of technological competence must increase. These guidelines are directed toward understanding the effects of scientific and technological issues on the lives of citizens in a global society.

Introduction to the Guidelines

This set of guidelines developed by the NCSS Science and Society Committee expands on the "Guidelines for Teaching Science-Related Social Issues" published in *Social Education* in April, 1983. A comparison of the two sets, however, shows substantial differences. These differences can be attributed to (1) an increased emphasis on and knowledge about technology in instruction and in our society; (2) a growing awareness of the interrelationships among science, technology, and society and their widespread effects on the lives of citizens in a global society; and (3) an increased body of data regarding teaching and learning for science and technology in the social studies (STS). These guidelines emphasize strong civic participation. The members of the Science and Society Committee believe that science, technology, and society (STS) instruction in the social studies must focus on citizenship participation. The definition of STS education and the guidelines themselves reflect this conviction.

The purposes of these guidelines parallel those of the original guidelines. These guidelines are intended to act as:

- a statement or position regarding the role and significance of social education in developing a competent, scientific, and technological citizenry;

- a starting point for expanding the dialogue on the nature, scope, goals, and methods of teaching about issues and topics related to science and technology within the context of the social education of students;
- a guide for schools and communities, teachers, departments, and school districts interested in introducing multidisciplinary programs, courses, mini-courses or units into existing social studies or science courses or building new courses that emphasize STS issues; and
- a baseline for assessing existing instructional programs and materials and for developing new program directions.

These guidelines focus on instruction about topics and issues that contain clear interrelationships among science, technology, and the social context in which they occur. The eight statements in 1.1 of the guidelines identify some of the characteristics of STS topics and issues in the social studies and provide the framework for the remainder of the guidelines.

The guidelines include suggestions for choosing topics or issues; identifying important content knowledge, values, thinking processes, and civic action applications to be taught; developing or selecting instructional techniques and strategies; assessing and evaluating teaching and learning success; and devising basic strategies for implementation.

Guidelines

1. **Choosing a Topic**
   1.1 Science, technology, society (STS) topics and lessons should focus on the social context in which they operate. Ideally, teachers should choose topics that:
      a. encourage learners to develop an understanding of themselves as interdependent members of society, and society as a responsible agent within the natural ecosystem;
      b. present clearly the mutual relationships and widespread effects of science, technology and society;
      c. present clearly the relationships and effects of scientific developments and new technologies to relevant issues on local or global scales;
      d. facilitate the presentation of a balance on differing viewpoints about issues and options and a critical review of the positions and sources of these viewpoints;
      e. provide opportunities for learners to develop and practice problem-solving and decision-making skills;
      f. provide opportunities for learners to apply the content, attitudes, and skills learned to responsible personal action and societal action or both;
      g. help and encourage learners to consider an expanded perspective on science, technology, and society including issues of personal and societal values and ethics; and
      h. foster confidence in the learners for handling science, technology, and society issues.
   1.2 Teachers must assess potential topics or units of study according to variables within the instructional setting such as:
      a. teacher background and expertise;
      b. resources available such as textbooks, videotapes, films, maps and atlases, artifacts, displays in local museums and outside resource persons;
      c. students' interests and concerns;
      d. social, emotional, cognitive levels and abilities of students;

e. relevance to courses of study or instructional goals of social studies and the instructional setting;
   f. sensitivities to the topic in the school and community;
   g. appropriateness to the age and developmental levels of learners; and
   h. selection of topics that are STS issues and worthy of examination.
1.3 Topics or lessons should have many entry points within the curriculum.
1.4 Topics or lessons should be dynamic; they should respond to current issues and problems and be relevant to the needs and interests of students.
1.5 Topics or lessons should build upon the current and relevant literature and issues, and the related work of professional organizations.
1.6 Topics or lessons should be interdisciplinary, i.e., geographical, historical, political, economic, legal, aesthetic, sociological, scientific, and ethical perspectives. They should require learners and teachers to apply knowledge, skills, and values learned in many content areas to science and technology issues and their effects on human existence.

2. **Knowledge of Content**

Teachers should help students to acquire knowledge about the following:

2.1 Science, technology, and society terms, concepts, and principles including:
   a. definitions of science, technology, and society;
   b. interactions and interdependence of science, technology, and society;
   c. nature of modern science and technology and their interrelationships with human existence from personal to global scales;
   d. increased dependency on technology in daily life;
   e. effects of emerging technologies on career choices;
   f. relationship of science and technology to the development of society and to our national and international heritage; and
   g. the interaction of the values and beliefs of a society and their effects on personal and public decision making regarding STS topics and issues.
2.2 Science, technology, society issues such as:
   a. nature of an STS issue and how to structure its components;
   b. sources of STS issues (local, state, national, and global levels);
   c. resources and their use (e.g., energy, food, materials, and land);
   d. political and social aspects of problems requiring the use of technology in their solution;
   e. human needs and aspirations (e.g., family and social relations, communications, food, clothing, transportation, commerce and industry, and work) and the relation of these to technological advancements; and
   f. effects of technology on local, state, national, and global levels.
2.3 Historical and geographical influences of society on science and technology and the resulting influences of science and technology on society;
2.4 Political and economic influences of science and technology and influences of science and technology on politics and economics;
2.5 Assessment and control of science and technology by individual choices and social mechanisms such as:
   a. role of technology and science assessment;
   b. nature of science and technology in public and social decision making;

c. roles of business and industry, government, and private sectors in policy making and the development of technology;

d. citizen influences: participation strategies for individuals and groups; and

e. roles and effects of mass communication, transportation, and medical advancements.

3. Values

The teacher will provide opportunities for students to learn and evaluate:

3.1 Value positions of groups and individuals in responding to science, technology and society-related issue definitions and resolutions;

3.2 The role of ethics and ethical responsibility in seeking resolutions to STS problems and issues;

3.3 Attitudes and beliefs of people regarding science and technology including personal and societal values, ethics, and how these affect the interaction of science, technology, and societal change;

3.4 Value positions as a source of unity or conflict within and among people and subsets of society;

3.5 Civic responsibility of an individual as an independent member of society, and society as a responsible agent within the natural ecosystem; and

3.6 The effects of values and ethics on the formation of public policy (how it is made, how it deals with topics or issues with special attention to the relationship between democratic values and STS issues).

4. Thinking Processes

Teachers will help learners to:

4.1 Develop models or frameworks that represent the complexity of the issue and the various perspectives, including historical, geographical, political, economic, legal, aesthetic, sociological, scientific, and ethical. These models or frameworks should be used to:

a. collect, analyze, and evaluate information and its sources; and

b. apply the information in rational and responsible problem solving and decision making.

4.2 Identify topics for investigation that expand critical thinking by:

a. defining and clarifying occasions for STS decisions (select issues or problems directly relevant to the learners whenever possible);

b. describing the situation or context giving rise to the problem or issue (e.g., political, economic, social, or physical causes);

c. identifying points of disagreement among individuals or groups; and

d. identifying alternatives and consequences to recommended actions.

4.3 Analyze STS topics and issues using stated criteria including but not limited to:

a. technological factor(s) present such as available resources (energy and materials), available human resources (numbers of individuals, skills) and available technologies;

b. social and physical conditions existing prior to the application of technology that can be affected by the application of technology;

c. science factors related to the technology and the relationship(s) such as genetic engineering and cryogenics;

d. intended results of the applications of technology and possible consequences (affected areas in regions or aspects of society);

e. benefits and costs of the application of technology; who gains and who pays economically or socially (individuals, groups, subsets of society, or society); and

f. values and value frameworks that entered into the decision to develop and use the technology such as the use of the atomic bomb at end of World War II.

4.4 Locate and process information to:

a. acquire information through careful analytic reading, listening, observing of material in mass media (television, newspapers, radio), interviews and presentations by authorities, computerized data bases, books, and other publications;

b. collect primary data through the design and use of interviews, questionnaires, rating scales, opinionnaires, and controlled observations;

c. develop basic science and technology vocabulary related to the issue, topic, or problem;

d. use and interpret pictures, charts, graphs, tables, and maps and use these tools to report findings to others;

e. locate and describe appropriate local, state, and national individuals, groups, agencies, and organizations that have a vested interest or regulatory responsibility regarding the problem or issue;

f. develop inquiry strategies that distinguish reliable and relevant information from unreliable and non-related information, identify the variables related to the issue or problem and that provide a sound basis for analysis and statement of conclusions;

g. develop concepts and generalizations supported by information; and

h. present and defend alternative solutions to problems or issues.

4.5 Evaluate information to:

a. distinguish fact from opinion;

b. compare information for supporting and contradicting arguments or data within one source and among a variety of sources;

c. recognize propaganda and bias and its purpose in a given context;

d. evaluate information received from media sources including media events, television coverage, videotapes, and computer programs;

e. evaluate the integrity of sources of information (e.g., expertise, vested interest) and the techniques used in these sources for collecting and reporting data; and

f. evaluate the relevance of the information to the issue or problem.

4.6 Work with others in solving problems, making decisions, or resolving controversy by:

a. interacting with individuals and groups that have differing points of view, alternative explanations, differing value orientations, and apparent power considerations or interests;

b. including strategies for discussion such as: formulating positions, including rationale, on STS issues or problems using supportive information that include empirical as well as value oriented data; communicating verbally and supporting a position on each issue; listening to the position and perspectives of those with opposing viewpoints; discussing the positions with others and negotiating a constructive resolution to conflicts; reaching a consensus, when possible, a joint position to which all sides can agree; and

c. predicating democratic decision making on group processes.

4.7 Use technologies (such as computers), whenever possible, in collecting, analyzing, and applying data.

4.8 Encourage the use of established problem-solving and decision-making models and computerized forecast models that organize and set priorities for information.

5. Civic Action

Teachers should assist students to:

5.1 Apply the knowledge, skills, and values learned to real situations that require responsible civic problem solving and decision making such as:
   a. in a school setting; and
   b. in the local community.

5.3 Identify present action plans that clearly illustrate the relation of science and technology to decisions about personal and social issues and problems.

5.2 Identify examples from history, the present day, and forecasts of the future that illustrate the importance of technologically competent citizens: those who can make informed judgments and rational decisions and can plan actions affecting human well-being, the national and global welfare, and the individual's quality of life.

5.4 Prepare an action plan, taking into consideration:
   a. formats for participation considering such concepts as consensus and trade-offs;
   b. alternatives and possible consequences based on empirical (cognitive and affective) information;
   c. relevance to values, beliefs, and behavior of self and significant others;
   d. goals of action plans;
   e. available resources and support; and
   f. evaluation of the action plan in a simulated setting.

5.5 Implement the plan.

5.6 Evaluate the results of the course of action including:
   a. collecting evidence related to action goals;
   b. evaluating the effectiveness and widespread effects on individuals, organizations, and groups;
   c. making value judgments about the results; and
   d. deciding whether to continue, modify the plan, or attempt alternate approaches.

6. Instructional Techniques and Strategies

Teachers should select and use materials and methods of instruction that consider the following:

6.1 Provide ample opportunities for knowledge, skills, and experience acquisition, development of values and attitudes, and participation in a social context.

6.2 Provide experiences that build on previous experiences and are consistent with the level of the learner's cognitive and social development.

6.3 Focus basic instructional strategies on active learning, taking into consideration:
   a. student participation in problem solving and decision making where learners experience the outcomes of plans and are responsible for them;
   b. opportunities for considering original data sources, integrity of data, and the separation of fact from fiction;

c. opportunities to explore diverse societal norms, individual perceptions of those norms, the influences of these norms on the formation of attitudes and values, and how these attitudes and values shape individual behavior toward scientific and technological issues;

d. teaching thinking skills as a part of the regular curriculum (teachers should give particular emphasis to thinking about those personal, cultural, and societal issues that influence the well-being of human beings); and

e. opportunities for students to engage in cooperative and collaborative activities.

6.4 Instructional methods and materials should include activities and devices such as:

a. direct and indirect experiences in various social contexts;

b. active participation in school and community activities;

c. indirect experiences through simulation, role playing, and simulation games and including emerging technologically-oriented hardware and software; and

d. use of present and emerging technology to obtain, interpret, and apply data to consider STS issues and problems. This should include hardware and software found in places such as classrooms, libraries, and laboratories.

6.5 Instruction should provide students with a clear focus on the relation of science and technology in historical, present-day, and future perspectives.

7. Assessment and Evaluation

In developing assessment and evaluation tools and procedures, the following should be important considerations:

7.1 The characteristics that distinguish STS lessons and topics from others (Section 1.1), should provide the primary focus for both the development of assessment and evaluation tools and procedures, and the goals for student learning.

7.2 Evaluation and criteria for student learning and instructional effectiveness should be based primarily on the statement of objectives by the respective school.

7.3 Expectations of students should be sensitive to cognitive, affective, and social developmental levels of students and to the social context of the local school district.

7.4 Assessment and evaluation should include both formative and summative techniques; those that measure on-going learning as well as long-term learning.

7.5 Assessment and evaluation should include a variety of techniques that assure higher order thinking, application skills, and affective learning as well as those that measure knowledge acquisition (e.g., decision making, civic participation). Examples of these techniques might include:

a. quizzes, examinations, and oral and written reports;

b. individual and group presentations by students that encourage the use of a variety of media;

c. interviews with students, both individually and in groups;

d. teacher observation and assessment of students during class activities using devices such as checklists and rating scales;

e. student presentations in and out of class;

f. technological devices (e.g., computers, video camera, video tape recorder);

g. student action plans and the implementation of these in the classroom or in an out-of-class social context; and

h. individual and group student projects, including dramatizations, forums or round table discussions, and role playing.

7.6 Assessment and evaluation should provide opportunities for expressing different student views, as long as relevant facts support them.

8. Implementation Strategies

The teacher should consider the following strategies for placing of lessons or units of instruction within the school curriculum:

8.1 Infusion into existing courses of study:
   a. adds content systematically and pervasively to courses on history, geography, and civics, for example;
   b. becomes an integral part of the existing curriculum; and
   c. omits some content in standard courses or may not identify STS content clearly when its effects are discussed.

8.2 Extension of existing units of study:
   a. adds STS content and activities to the end of lessons in traditional social studies courses;
   b. permits the extension and applications of traditional social studies content;
   c. has the advantage of maximum flexibility in placement and length of STS content; and
   d. can result in superficial and unsystematic treatment of STS content.

8.3 Creation of separate courses of study:
   a. tends to be interdisciplinary or multidisciplinary in content;
   b. permits systematic and sustained study of various interrelationships of science, technology, and society; and
   c. may include the main disadvantages of difficulty in achieving sustained school support or constant challenges to organizing course content from various academic disciplines.

8.4 Awareness of STS conceptual framework for learners by emphasizing STS content already included in standard curricula, i.e., American history courses. It would be beneficial if technological and scientific events were identified as such when their effects were discussed.

References

Aikenhead, Glen. "The Content of STS Education." *A Missive to the Science-Technology-Society Research Network* 2 (July 1986):18-23.

Bybee, Roger, and Teri Mau. "Science and Technology-Related Global Problems: An International Survey of Science Educators." *Journal of Research in Science Teaching* 23 (July 1986): 599-618.

Hamlen, Patrick. "Science, Technology and Politics: The Literature." *Teaching Political Science* 14 (Summer 1982): 158-162.

Heath, Phillip A. "Science/Technology/Society in the Social Studies." *ERIC Digest EDO-SO-88-8*. Bloomington, Ind.: Clearinghouse for Social Studies/Social Science Education, 1988.

Hickman, Faith, John Patrick, and Roger Bybee. *Science/Technology/Society: A Framework for Curriculum Reform in Secondary Science and Social Studies*. Boulder, Colo.: Social Science Education Consortium, 1987.

Hofstein, Ari, and Robert Yager. "Societal Issues as Organizers for Science Education in the '80s." *School Science and Mathematics* 82 (November 1982): 539-547.

Otto, Robert. "How To Do It: Teaching Science-Related Social Issues." *Social Education* 51 (April/May 1987): 1-4.

Otto, Robert A., ed. "Implementation of the NCSS Guidelines for Teaching Science-Related Social Issues." *Resources in Education* (September 1987): 77.

Patrick, John, and Richard Remy. *Connecting Science, Technology, and Society in the Education of Citizens*. Boulder, Colo.: Social Science Education Consortium, 1985.

Patrick, John, and Richard Remy. "Crossing Two Cultures in the Education of Citizens." *American Biology Teacher* 44 (September 1982): 346-350.

Rubba, Peter. "Perspectives on Science-Technology-Society Instruction." *School Science and Mathematics* 87 (March 1987): 181-186.

Science and Society Committee of the National Council for the Social Studies. "Guidelines for Teaching Science-Related Social Issues." *Social Education* 47 (April 1983): 258-261.

Solomon, Joan. "Science and Society Studies in the School Curriculum." *Social Science Review* 62 (December 1980): 213-219.

Contributors to this statement include: Phillip Heath, Ohio State University, Lima; Fred Splittgerber, University of South Carolina, Columbia; Gerald Marker, Indiana University, Bloomington; Barbara Barchi, The Pennsylvania State University, University Park; Charles White, George Mason University, Fairfax, Virginia; John Patrick, Indiana University, Bloomington; and David Seiter, Davis County School System, Utah.

Curriculum Documents in ERIC: A Select Annotated Bibliography for Social Studies Educators

Curriculum Documents in ERIC: A Select Annotated Bibliography for Social Studies Educators

John J. Patrick and C. Frederick Risinger

The 1980s were years of great concern about the curricula of elementary and secondary schools. Throughout the past decade educators in the social studies, and in other fields of knowledge, formed curriculum study projects to assess the status quo and recommend improvements in widely distributed reports. The major curriculum reform reports can be found in the database of ERIC, the Educational Resources Information Center.

This select bibliography is the product of a systematic search of the ERIC database to identify documents on social studies curriculum reform projects of the 1980s. Some items in the following list exemplify curriculum reform efforts in particular subjects of the social studies, such as history, geography, economics, and international studies. Other documents are examples of comprehensive curriculum reforms in social studies from kindergarten through grade twelve.

Most of these ERIC documents are products of short-term curriculum study groups or commissions, such as the National Commission on Social Studies in the Schools, the Bradley Commission on History in Schools, or the Education for Democracy Project of the American Federation of Teachers. A few documents were developed and distributed by the U.S. Department of Education, such as *A Nation At Risk*. This bibliography also includes a small number of curriculum frameworks or course guides developed by state-level departments of education, such as the "California History-Social Science Framework," the "Utah Core Curriculum Standards," the "Texas Social Studies Framework," and the "New York Social Studies Program." The state curriculum documents in this list are merely a few of the many state-level education department materials in the ERIC database. They do, however, reflect the great variety of these types of documents that can be found through a search of the ERIC database.

One of the more significant resources related to curriculum reform in the social studies is the November/December 1986 issue of *Social Education* (Volume 50, Number 7). In a special section, six alternative scope and sequence models were proposed. Following an introduction by then-NCSS President Donald Bragaw, each of the six curriculum models is described. Subsequently, an *ad hoc* committee called for by the NCSS House of Delegates evaluated and recommended three of the models to the NCSS Board of Directors for official endorsement. The Board approved the recommendation in September 1988.

The ERIC system includes each of the six models with a separate EJ number. The authors and EJ numbers are: (1) Dynneson and Gross, (EJ 343 078); (2) Downey, (EJ 343 079); (3) Hartoonian and Laughlin, (EJ 343 080); (4) Engle and Ochoa, (EJ 343 081); (5) Stanley and Nelson, (EJ 343 082); and (6) Kneip, (EJ 343 083). *Social Education* is available in many college and school libraries and article reprints are also available from the UMI Article Clearinghouse, University Microfilms International, 300 North Zeeb Road, Box 91, Ann Arbor, MI 48106.

In addition to the curriculum frameworks, models, and guidelines in this bibliography, there are four recently released documents on assessments of learners. Three documents are the National Assessment of Educational Progress (NAEP) reports on geography, history, and civics. The fourth document reports a national assessment of learning in economics, which was produced by the Joint Council on Economic Education.

The ERIC documents in this select bibliography may be purchased from the ERIC Document Reproduction Service (EDRS), 3900 Wheeler Avenue, Alexandria, VA 22304-6409; telephone numbers are (800) 227-3742 and (703) 823-0500. All the documents are available in microfiche (MF), and some are also available in paper copy (PC). Contact EDRS about prices. Use the ED numbers in this bibliography to identify documents you want to obtain from EDRS. EDRS accepts major credit cards and will even provide fax service and overnight delivery.

The documents in the bibliography that follows are indicative of the many other curriculum documents that can be found in the ERIC database. Additional social studies curriculum documents can be found by searching the *Resources in Education* (RIE) index, produced monthly by the U.S. Department of Education. The *RIE* indexes are available in more than 850 libraries throughout the United States. These libraries may also have a complete collection of ERIC documents on microfiche for viewing or copying. Curriculum documents in ERIC may also be located through a computer search of the ERIC database.

The following list of descriptors (ERIC subject headings) can be used to do a computer search of ERIC or to find documents in the *RIE* index.

List of ERIC Descriptors on Social Studies Curriculum Reform

- Academic Achievement
- Citizenship Education
- Civics
- Cognitive Development
- Core Curriculum
- Course Content
- Curriculum Development
- Curriculum Guides
- Economics
- Educational Change
- Educational Objectives
- Educational Quality
- Elementary School Curriculum
- Elementary Secondary Instruction
- Guidelines
- Geography Instruction
- Global Approach
- History
- History Instruction
- Instructional Improvement
- International Education
- Program Improvement
- Role of Education
- School Effectiveness
- Secondary Curriculum
- Sequential Approach
- Social Sciences
- Social Studies
- State Curriculum Guides
- State Standards
- Textbook Content
- Textbook Evaluation
- U.S. History
- World Geography
- World History

Select Bibliography

Allen, Russell et al. *The Geographic Learning of High School Seniors.* Princeton, NJ: National Assessment of Educational Progress, Educational Testing Service, 1990. ED 313 317. (Paper copy also available from the National Assessment of Educational Progress, Educational Testing Service, Rosedale Road, Princeton, NJ 08541-0001, $10.00.)

This report presents results of the 1988 National Assessment of Educational Progress (NAEP) survey of the geographic knowledge and skills of high school seniors. A national stratified sample of more than 3,000 twelfth graders from 300 public and private schools responded to seventy-six multiple-choice questions about four topics in geography: (1) knowing locations, such as countries, cities, and physical places; (2) using the skills and tools of geography, such as map and globe symbols and longitude and latitude; (3) understanding cultural geography, including human-environment relationships and cultural change; and (4) understanding physical geography, including climate, weather, tectronics, and erosion. The results indicate that students generally are deficient in geographic knowledge and skills. This problem may be associated with inadequate treatment of geography in the high school curriculum. Much of the geography presented to high school students is integrated with courses in history and science. Less than two-thirds of these respondents had taken a high school course in geography. There was no relationship, however, between taking geography coursework and better performance on this test. But students who studied geography in a U.S. history course performed better than those without this academic experience. Better performance on this test was linked to certain background factors, such as well-educated parents, both parents living at home, availability of many reading materials, limited viewing of television, and time spent doing homework.

American Federation of Teachers. *Education for Democracy: A Statement of Principles. Guidelines for Strengthening the Teaching of Democratic Values.* Washington, D.C.: American Federation of Teachers, 1987. ED 313 217. (Paper copy also available from the American Federation of Teachers, 555 New Jersey Avenue, NW, Washington, DC 20001—first copy free; additional copies, $2.50 each.)

Based on the premise that democracy's values will not survive if they are not purposefully transmitted to successive generations, this booklet proposes that U.S. schools increase efforts to improve citizenship education. The featured issues are: (1) the reasons improvements are needed; (2) what citizens need to know; and (3) the role of humanities and history instruction as the core of democratic education. The booklet concludes that there is a need for: (1) the teaching of a more demanding social studies curriculum; (2) a reordering of curricula around history and geography; (3) the using of enhanced imagination in history instruction; (4) increasing global studies; and (5) offering more humanities instruction, especially in literature, ideas, and biography. A major curriculum reform effort will require more effective textbooks and resource materials, collaboration between schools and universities, and new approaches to teacher education.

Anderson, Lee et al. *The Civics Report Card: Trends in Achievement from 1976 to 1988 at Ages 13 and 17; Achievement in 1988 at Grades 4, 8, and 12.* Princeton, N.J.: National Assessment of Educational Progress, Educational Testing Service, 1990. ED 315 376. (Paper copy also available from NAEP, Educational Testing Service, Rosedale Road, Princeton, NJ 08541-0001, $10.00.)

This report summarizes findings from two national surveys of U.S. civics achievement conducted by the National Assessment of Educational Progress. Part 1 reports on a trend assessment of students at ages thirteen and seventeen, carried out during the 1975-76, 1981-82, and 1987-88 school years. Chapter 1 summarizes national trends, trends for demographic subpopulations, trends in students' ability to define democracy, and trends in students' ability to identify the value of multiple newspaper publishers. Part 2 reports on patterns of achievement of fourth, eighth, and twelfth-grade students in 1988. Chapter 2 summarizes the levels of civics proficiency across the grades. Chapter 3 compares civics proficiency across subpopulations defined by gender, race and ethnicity, region, and other characteristics. Chapter 4 explores students' performances in specific content areas such as democratic principles and the purpose of government, political processes, and rights, responsibilities, and the law. Chapter 5 describes the amount of instruction students reported receiving in civics, while chapter 6 discusses the topics studied and the instructional approaches used in these classes. Appendices contain procedural information and tables of statistical data that supplement the information in the text.

Bennett, William J. *James Madison Elementary School: A Curriculum for American Students.* Washington, D.C.: U.S. Department of Education, 1988. ED 295 760.

Former Secretary of Education William Bennett's personal recommendations for a sound elementary school core curriculum are presented by means of a report on a fictional "James Madison Elementary School." The report opens with discussion of the importance of commitment to course content and instruction in basic skills in elementary schools, the necessity of integrating content in elementary curriculum, and obstacles that may face implementation of the core curriculum. A chart outlining the program's educational goals precedes a more detailed description of the proposed program, which is for grades kindergarten through eight. Discussion focuses on the current status and suggested goals by grade for English, social studies (history, geography, and civics), mathematics, science, foreign language, fine arts, and physical education and health. Suggested reading lists (with emphasis on classics of children's literature) for grades K-3, 4-6, and 7-8 are provided in the English section. Included after the discussion of each subject area are profiles of curricular excellence from actual programs around the United States.

Bennett, William J. *James Madison High School: A Curriculum for American Students.* Washington, D.C.: U.S. Department of Education, 1987. ED 287 854.

This document presents former Secretary of Education William Bennett's personal concept of a sound secondary school core curriculum. It is called "James Madison High School" in honor of President James Madison and his strong views that the people, in order to govern properly, must arm themselves with knowledge. The theoretical curriculum consists of four years of English, and three years each of social studies, mathematics, and science, two years each of foreign language and physical education, and a half-year each of art and music. A brief discussion is offered on the desirability of a curriculum that makes available a shared body of knowledge and skills, a common language of ideas, and a common moral and intellectual discipline. A chart describing the four-year plan of the program shows the number of years required for each core subject and the names of the courses that fulfill them. To demonstrate the flexibility of the program, sample schedules for three students pursuing different goals are outlined. Profiles of seven exemplary high school programs provide an insight into what is currently being accomplished with rigorous core curriculums. The profiled schools, each serving students of diverse backgrounds, are: (1) A. Philip Randolph Campus High School (New York); (2) CAL High School (Iowa); (3) James A. Garfield High School (California); (4) Shawnee Mission South High School (Kansas); (5) Portland High School (Maine); (6) Xavier Prep School (Louisiana); and (7) Wayland High School (Massachusetts).

Bradley Commission on History in Schools. *Building a History Curriculum: Guidelines for Teaching History in the Schools.* Washington, D.C.: Educational Excellence Network, 1988. ED 310 008. (Paper copy available from the Bradley Commission on History in Schools, 29615 Westwood Road, Suite A-2, Westlake, OH 44145, and the Educational Excellence Network, 1112 Sixteenth Street, NW, Suite 500, Washington, DC 20036, $3.00.)

The Bradley Commission on History in Schools was created in 1987 in response to concern over the inadequacy of the history taught in U.S. elementary and secondary classrooms. These history curriculum guidelines were designed by the Bradley Commission to help those responsible for making curriculum decisions realize the manifest importance of developing and maintaining a vigorous history curriculum. The Commission recommends that: (1) historical studies should focus on thematic context and chronological perspective to develop critical judgment capabilities; (2) the curricular time required to develop genuine understanding in history programs be considerably greater than that currently allowed; (3) the K-6 social studies curriculum be history-centered; (4) no fewer than four years of history be required between grades seven and twelve; (5) this curriculum should include the historical experiences of peoples from all parts of the world and all constituent parts of those societies; and (6) a substantial program of history, with suitable structure and content, be required for certification of social studies teachers in middle and high schools. Thirty-two topics are suggested for the study of U.S. history, world civilization, and western civilization. Curricular patterns or course sequences are presented for both K-6 (three patterns) and middle and high schools (four patterns). Criteria for the examination of the structure, priority, and content of courses are also given.

California State Department of Education. *History/Social Science Framework for California Public Schools.* Sacramento: California State Department of Education, 1988. ED 293 779. (Paper copy available only from Bureau of Educational Sales, California State Department of Education, P.O. Box 271, Sacramento, CA 95802-0271, $6.00.)

This framework, centered in the chronological study of history, proposes an integrated and correlated approach to the teaching of history and the social sciences. The framework is structured around three major goals, each comprising several curriculum strands which are to be developed from kindergarten through grade twelve. The three goals are: (1) knowledge and cultural understanding; (2) democratic understanding and cultural values; and (3) skills attainment and social participation. The programs for kindergarten through the third grade are: (1) "Learning and Working Now and Long Ago"; (2) "A Child's Place in Time and Space"; (3) "People Who Make a Difference"; and (4) "Continuity and Change." State history is taught in the fourth grade. Fifth graders study U.S. history from the pre-Columbian period through 1850. The sixth-grade program is developed around the ancient world to

A.D. 500. The medieval and early modern world through 1789 are presented in grade seven, setting the context for the study of U.S. history from 1783 to 1914 in grade eight. The modern world from 1789 to the present is studied in grade ten. The eleventh grade provides an in-depth study of the United States from 1900 to the present. Students choose electives in grade nine from a variety of courses. The culminating courses are principles of U.S. democracy and economics in grade twelve. Criteria for evaluating instructional materials are provided.

Curriculum Task Force of the National Commission on Social Studies in the Schools. *Charting a Course: Social Studies for the 21st Century*. Washington, D.C.: National Commission on Social Studies in the Schools, 1989. ED number to be assigned. (Also available from the National Council for the Social Studies, 3501 Newark Street, NW, Washington, DC 20016, $7.00 plus $2.00 postage and handling.)

Part 1 of this report covers the recommended social studies curriculum for grades K-12. Part 2 discusses the research basis for curriculum choice. Part 3 contains essays prepared by representatives of the professional associations holding membership in the Social Science Association's Task Force for Pre-College Education. These essays provide a perspective from the following fields: (1) anthropology; (2) economics; (3) U.S. history; (4) world history; (5) political science; (6) psychology; and (7) sociology. The characteristics of a social studies curriculum for the 21st century as set forth in this report include the following: (1) It must instill a clear understanding of the roles of citizens in a democracy and provide opportunities for active, engaged participation in civic, cultural, and volunteer activities. (2) It must provide consistent and cumulative learning from kindergarten through grade twelve. (3) History and geography should provide the matrix for social studies with concepts from political science, economics, and other social sciences integrated throughout the curriculum. (4) A global approach should be taken, for a curriculum that focuses on one or two major civilizations is neither adequate nor complete. (5) Integration of other subject matter with social studies should be encouraged. (6) Students must be made aware that they have the capacity to shape the future. (7) Teaching strategies should help students become both independent and cooperative learners who develop skills of problem solving, decision making, negotiation, and conflict resolution. (8) Learning materials must incorporate a rich mix of written matter, audiovisual materials, computer programs, and items of material culture.

Gagnon, Paul. *Democracy's Half-told Story: What American History Textbooks Should Add*. Washington, D.C.: American Federation of Teachers, 1989. ED 313 305. (Paper copy also available from the Education for Democracy Project, American Federation of Teachers, 555 New Jersey Avenue, NW, Washington, DC 20001, $7.00 for 1-10 copies; additional copies $5.00.)

The first purpose of a high school course in U.S. history must be to help students understand the essence of democracy and those events, institutions, and forces that have either promoted or obstructed it. This review examines five textbooks and analyzes how useful they are in aiding that process, and how they might be made more helpful. The five texts are: (1) "A History of the United States" (D. Boorstin; B. Kelley); (2) "History of a Free People" (H. Bragdon; S. McCutchen); (3) "The United States: A History of the Republic" (J. Davidson; M. Lytle); (4) "People and Our Country" (N. Risjord; T. Haywoode); and (5) "Triumph of the American Nation" (L. Todd; M. Curti). The texts are reviewed using topic divisions such as: "History's Role in Civic Education"; "Old World Backgrounds"; "Civil

War and Emancipation"; "Change and Reform Before World War I"; and "Depression, New Deal, and War Again." The textbooks under review are at one and the same time over-detailed and under-detailed: the first, because they try to mention something about everything; the second, because they fail to develop major themes in depth. They labor too hard to balance affirmation and negation of U.S. history, and the result is a detached neutrality, passionless about both the ugly and the beautiful moments in that history. The texts should convey the complication, drama, suspense, and the paradox of comedy and tragedy found in history. The Education for Democracy Project's Statement of Principles and its signatories are given in the appendix.

Gagnon, Paul. *Democracy's Untold Story: What World History Textbooks Neglect.* Washington, D.C.: American Federation of Teachers, 1987. ED 313 268. (Paper copy also available from the Education for Democracy Project, American Federation of Teachers, 555 New Jersey Avenue, NW, Washington, DC 20001, $4.98.)

Content weakness in textbooks is a major obstacle to effective social studies teaching. Chapters 1-3 of this book provide the Education for Democracy Project's Statement of Principles, a consideration of history's role as the core of social studies education, and the role of textbooks in teaching world history. Chapters 4-14 examine five selected world history textbooks in terms of included information about and treatment of: (1) the purpose of history instruction; (2) the Greek legacy; (3) Rome's fall and legacy; (4) Judaism's and Christianity's basic ideas; (5) the Middle Ages as a source of representative government; (6) the 17th century English Parliament; (7) ideas from the Enlightenment; (8) the American and French Revolutions; (9) major ideas of the 19th century; (10) nation-states, nationalism, and imperialism; (11) World War I; (12) totalitarianism; (13) U.S. foreign policy; and (14) democracy in the world since 1945. This book concludes that these world history textbooks tend to neglect democracy's ideas, principles, origins, needs, and significance and that, when included, these concepts are not systematically presented. Teachers may not be able to rely on world history textbooks to convey and teach the concepts of struggles for freedom, self-government, and justice.

Gardner, David P. et al. *A Nation at Risk: The Imperative for Education Reform.* Washington, D.C.: National Commission on Excellence in Education, 1983. ED 226 006. (Paper copy also available from Superintendent of Documents, Government Office, Washington, DC 20402, Stock No. 065-000-00177-2, $4.50.)

This report: (1) investigates the declining state of the educational system in America, as measured by high school student performance in the United States and other countries; (2) identifies specific problem areas; and (3) offers multiple recommendations for improvement. The five major recommendations arrived at appear, respectively, under the headings: content, standards and expectations, time, teaching, leadership and fiscal support. Recommendations pertaining to content include the strengthening of high school graduation requirements by establishing minimum requirements for each student of: (a) four years of English; (b) three years of mathematics; (c) three years of science; (d) three years of social studies; and (e) one-half year of computer science. With regard to standards and expectations, schools, colleges, and universities are encouraged to adopt more rigorous and measurable standards and higher expectations for academic performance and student conduct. Four-year colleges and universities, in particular, are advised to raise their admission requirements. In order to improve time usage, the report advises that more time should be devoted to students learning the "New Basics," which may, in turn, require a longer school day, or a lengthened school year. Seven ways to improve teacher preparation and to make teaching a more rewarding and respected profession are listed. Six implementation guidelines are suggested for improving educational leadership and fiscal support. Appendices contain: (a) charter of the National Commission on Excellence in Education; (b) schedule of the Commission's public events; (c) list of commissioned papers; (d) list of individuals who testified at Commission hearings; (e) list of other presentations to the Commission; and (f) notable programs.

Hammack, David C. et al. *The U.S. History Report Card: The Achievement of Fourth, Eighth, and Twelfth-grade Students in 1988 and Trends from 1986 to 1988 in the Factual Knowledge of High School Juniors*. Princeton, N.J.: National Assessment of Educational Progress, Educational Testing Service, 1990. ED 315 377. (Paper copy also available from NAEP, Educational Testing Service, Rosedale Road, Princeton, NJ 08541-0001, $10.00.)

Each of the three parts of this report provides a somewhat different perspective on U.S. students' knowledge and understanding of U.S. history. Part 1 summarizes the assessment performance of fourth, eighth, and twelfth-grade students based on the National Assessment of Educational Progress history proficiency scale. Chapter 1 uses this measure to summarize the levels of proficiency displayed by students in the 1988 assessment, offering an overview and examples of their knowledge and understandings. Chapter 2 compares U.S. history proficiency across the grades and across subpopulations defined by race and ethnicity, gender, region, and other characteristics. Part 2 of the report takes a closer look at the assessment results. The chapters in this section provide information not only on the results of the assessment of students in grades four, eight, and twelve, but also on trends in the performance of eleventh-grade students, based on a special study conducted in 1986 and 1988. Chapter 3 explores students' knowledge of historical periods, chronology, documents, and persons, while chapter 4 summarizes their familiarity with the historical contexts of political and economic life as well as of cultural, social, and family life. Part 3 describes the amount and nature of social studies and U.S. history instruction reported by students who participated in the 1988 assessment and in the special trend assessment. Chapter 5 summarizes the extent of students' instruction in these subjects, and chapter 6 reports on various aspects of this instruction—particularly the topics studied and the prevalence of various instructional activities. Many tables of statistical data are included.

Hartoonian, H. Michael. *A Guide to Curriculum Planning in Social Studies Education*. Madison, Wisc.: Wisconsin State Department of Public Instruction, 1986. ED 268 038.

Designed to provide social studies educators with specific information for the development of local school district K-12 curriculum, this guide is organized into eight sections. Following an introduction, section 1 provides a rationale, goals, and major themes for the social studies and social sciences. Section 2 presents a scope and sequence organization by grade level. Section 3 examines thinking and reasoning as educational objectives and presents a rationale for an "Integrated Skills Network." Section 4, which focuses on evaluating and improving the social studies program, is followed by a discussion of the use of computers and software in the social studies. In section 6, resources and references for teachers are listed including professional organizations, information sources, and books for the social studies professional. Section 7 examines the changing curriculum, limitations of textbooks in an information age, the coordinating of schooling and education, the remodeling of the structure of knowledge and logic, balancing the fragmenting and binding forces of schooling, and the radical reconstruction of education. Appendices (section 8) provide information on graduation requirements, minimum allocated instructional time, writing in the social studies, the Directed Reading/Thinking Activity (DRTA), state social studies publications and observance days, instructional television programs, and the use of informal classroom drama.

Hertzberg, Hazel Whitman. *Social Studies Reform, 1880-1980*. Boulder, Colo.: Social Science Education Consortium, Inc., 1981. ED 211 429. (Paper copy also available from Social Science Education Consortium, Inc., 3300 Mitchell Lane, Suite 240, Boulder, CO 80302, $12.95)

The purposes, methodologies, and curricula of the social studies over the past 100 years are examined in this paper. This history was written to provide a useful background for current efforts to reform the social studies. The paper, which consists of nine chapters, begins with a discussion of the meanings, definitions, and beginnings of social studies. The three factors that set the stage for the development of the social studies are examined: the rise of the public high school, the growth of the universities, and the emergence of professional societies. Chapter two examines the 1916 report and the 1920s. The American Historical Association (AHA) Commission on the social studies and the 1930s are treated in chapter three. Chapter four examines the effect that World War II had on the social studies. The "New Social Studies" movement is the topic of chapters five, six, and seven. What happened in the 1970s is discussed in chapter eight. Following the summary and comments of chapter nine, there are name and subject indexes.

Iowa State Department of Public Instruction. *A Guide to Curriculum Development in Social Studies*. Des Moines: Iowa State Department of Public Instruction, 1986. ED 280 783.

Designed to aid teachers and administrators in developing curriculum and improving instruction in the K-12 social studies, this guide is intended to help districts enhance and build upon their current local curriculum. It is also designed to assist educators in developing social studies programs to meet children's educational needs. The guide is organized into three major sections: (1) rationale, philosophy, and goals; (2) scope, sequence, and strategies which include democratic beliefs and values, skills, approaches to organizing instruction, suggested teaching and learning strategies, sample lesson formats, and course descriptions; and (3) evaluation, which covers student and program evaluation as well as the selection of evaluation materials. The appendices include samples of general objectives for social studies and skills; sample allocation of instructional time in elementary schools; needs assessment instruments; computers, software, and the social studies; and a curriculum planning model for the K-12 social studies. Figures and tables are also part of the appendices.

Joint Committee on Geographic Education. *Guidelines for Geographic Education: Elementary and Secondary Schools*. Washington, D.C.: Association of American Geographers, 1984. ED 252 453. (Paper copy only available from the Association of American Geographers, 1710 Sixteenth Street, NW, Washington, DC 20009 or the National Council for Geographic Education, Indiana University of Pennsylvania, 1-B Leonard Hall, Indiana, PA 15705, $3.00.)

Intended as a current statement for improving geographic education, these guidelines suggest major changes needed to counteract a prevailing illiteracy in geography among U.S. citizens. A preface and problem statement provide a rationale for including geography education as a subject of study in the schools and as a scientific mode of inquiry. A section on the content and process of geographic education (1) demonstrates how geographic education focuses on five central themes (location, place, relationships within places, movement, and regions), how these themes recur and are amplified throughout the curriculum, and how they should be represented in the various levels of our schools; (2) suggests how schools can integrate these themes; (3) identifies the knowledge, skills, and perspectives students should gain from a systematic program in geographic education; and (4) suggests a variety of approaches to geography that each theme might imply. The following section, "The Place of Geography in the Curriculum," deals with the value of geographic inquiry, geography's relationship to other subjects, and geography as preparation for a career. In the next section, a chart depicting the role and sequence of geography education in the elementary school presents central foci and suggested learning outcomes by grade level. A suggested pattern of course offerings and sequence for geographic education in the secondary school is followed by an outline of skills to be included in high school geography courses and a list of learning outcomes arranged according to the five basic themes identified earlier in the guidelines.

New Jersey State Department of Education. *World History/Cultures Guide.* Trenton, N.J.: New Jersey State Department of Education, 1988. ED 312 169. (Paper copy also available from New Jersey State Department of Education, 225 West State Street, CN 500, Trenton, NJ 08625, $3.25.)

In 1988-89, a one-year course in world history/cultures was added to the list of courses required for graduation in the state of New Jersey, becoming the third required course in social studies. The course is intended to provide students with historical knowledge to better meet the demands of the world and to make the informed decisions that are so crucial to a democratic way of life. This curriculum guide is designed to stimulate multiple perspectives in the development, modification, and evaluation of such a course. The guide includes a statement of philosophy; a rationale for a world history/cultures course; curriculum guidelines; course objectives; five curriculum approaches; a 27-item resource list of agencies and organizations that could provide more information; an 8-item bibliography, and a feedback form. Course objectives are discussed in terms of knowledge, skills, attitudes, and social participation; each of the objectives are broken down into additional goals and objectives. The five curriculum approaches (two examples of each approach are given) are world history, world cultures, world geography, global studies, and international relations.

New York State Education Department. *Social Studies Program, 1987 Updated Edition.* Albany, N.Y.: New York State Education Department, 1987. ED 287 788.

The goals for this social studies curriculum are the development of essential concepts, skills, and content that have been identified for the social studies program. The curriculum was designed to meet student needs and interests, to reflect increasing knowledge about child development and learning, and to give attention to the learning environment as well as the course content. It also attempts to educate for multicultural understanding and cooperation in an increasingly interdependent world. Key concepts are (1) change, (2) citizenship, (3) culture, (4) empathy, (5) environment, (6) identity, (7) interdependence, (8) nation-state, (9) scarcity, and (10) technology. Content understanding, learning activities, skill development, evaluation, and resources are given for each of the ten concepts. Strategies for linking children's literature with social studies are presented. Examples of participation projects and guidelines for development are provided and teachers are encouraged to participate with students to plan K-6 classroom projects. General content understandings are given for each of the K-6 grade levels.

Nicolosi, Louis J. et al. *World Geography Curriculum Guide: Secondary Social Studies*. Baton Rouge, La.: Louisiana State Department of Education, 1985. ED 295 884.

This world geography curriculum guide is designed to help teachers improve the quality of secondary level geography instruction. The guide contains Louisiana's social studies curriculum goals and information about the scope and sequence of the state's social studies program. Part 1 discusses the major geographical concepts of: (1) map and globe skills; (2) physical geography; (3) changing landscapes; (4) natural resources; (5) population; (6) living off the land; and (7) urban studies. Part 2 uses these concepts in units about (1) Western Europe; (2) Eastern Europe; (3) Anglo America; (4) Latin America; (5) North Africa and the Middle East; (6) Africa south of the Sahara; (7) Asia; (8) the Pacific region; and (9) the Polar regions. One country from each region is featured, and each unit contains generalizations, concept and objectives statements, along with a general course content outline and suggested student activities. Appendices include: (1) a 62-item bibliography; (2) a list of foreign countries' embassies and information offices in the United States; (3) charts showing skills for grades K-12 according to whether they constitute a major or shared responsibility of social studies; and (4) a description of course evaluation techniques.

North Carolina State Department of Education. *Social Studies Grades K-12. North Carolina Competency Based Curriculum*. Raleigh, N.C.: North Carolina State Department of Education, 1985. ED 270 343.

A scope and sequence for teaching elementary and secondary social studies is provided in a subject-by-subject format. Designed to meet the requirements of North Carolina's competency-based curriculum, materials may also be useful to other states and localities. Following a foreword and acknowledgments, material is divided into three main sections. A background and overview contains an introduction and discusses philosophy and rationale, the role of thinking skills in the social studies curriculum, programs for exceptional children, and how to read the teacher handbook. The bulk of the document is presented in a section entitled "Social Studies Competency-Based Curriculum." Introductory material for this section includes a description of purpose, overview, and learning outcomes. Subsections are organized by the following grade levels: grades K-3, 4-6, 7-8, and 9-12. Within each subsection, major emphases and theme, knowledge, and skills for each grade level are presented individually in matrix format. Grade level themes are: grade one, the individual and group relationships; grade two, home and school; grade three, communities; grade four, North Carolina; grade five, the Western hemisphere; grade six, the Eastern hemisphere (Europe and the Soviet Union); grade seven, the Eastern hemisphere (Africa and Asia); grade eight, North Carolina history; grade nine, economic, political, and legal systems; grade ten, world studies; and grade eleven, United States history. Included in the nine appendices are materials on the Elementary and Secondary School Reform Act of 1984, the Standard Course of Study (North Carolina Administrative Code), the course requirements for high school graduation, the North Carolina Scholars Program, the secondary level testing requirements, and the textbook adoption prices in North Carolina.

Parker, Walter C. *Renewing the Social Studies Curriculum*. Alexandria, Va. ASCD, In Press (ED number forthcoming).

This book concerns the art of curriculum deliberation in the field of social studies. Its audience is the local curriculum planning committee. Its themes are democratic education in a multicultural society and challenging lessons on essential learnings. The first chapter discusses the first theme and suggests five essential learnings. The second places curriculum planning in its social settings: school organization, the community, and, broadly, the present North American milieux. The third presents a case study of two curriculum renewal meetings of a school district curriculum planning committee. The fourth presents three general principles to guide curriculum renewal in social studies, an eight-part renewal model, and pitfalls to be avoided. The fifth describes the typical social studies curriculum in the U.S. today along with alternatives, issues, and trends. The final chapter advocates and examines two trends: authentic assessments and in-depth study on a limited number of essential topics.

Saunders, Phillip et al. *Master Curriculum Guide in Economics: A Framework for Teaching the Basic Concepts*. 2d Edition. New York: Joint Council on Economic Education, 1984. ED 247 198. (Paper copy available only from the Joint Council on Economic Education, 432 Park Avenue South, New York, NY 10016, $5.00.)

Intended for curriculum developers, this revised Framework presents a set of basic concepts for teaching K-12 economics. The revision reflects the change and development which the field of economics has undergone and includes improvements suggested by users of the first edition. The purpose of teaching economics is to impart a general understanding of how our economy works and to improve economic decision making by students through the use of an orderly, reasoned approach. Chapters I, II, and III provide a brief introduction to the publication, discuss the elements of economic understanding, and list and describe some basic economic concepts. Chapter IV discusses the broad social goals that seem most important in the United States today, the problem of trade-offs among goals, and the role of self-interest and personal values. Chapter V illustrates the use of a decision-making model with two economic issues involving public policy. The concluding chapter, chapter VI, discusses the grade placement of the economic concepts.

Study Commission on Global Education. *The United States Prepares for its Future: Global Perspectives in Education*. New York: Global Perspectives in Education, Inc., 1987. ED 283 758. (Paper copy also available from The American Forum, 45 John Street, Suite 1200, New York, NY 10038, $10.00 plus postage.)

This report addresses the question of what knowledge and skills should be taught to citizens whose judgment is the ultimate source of policy in a democratic nation. The report recommends the adoption of new goals for school programs, changes in curriculum offerings and in teacher education, creation of curriculum development centers, greater cooperation among schools and universities, and increased support and cooperation from the private sector. The report further recommends that every subject area in primary and secondary schools be approached from a global perspective, and that four curricular areas be emphasized: (1) an understanding of the world as a series of interrelated systems; (2) increased attention to the development of world civilizations as they relate to the history of the United States; (3) greater attention to diversity of cultural patterns; and (4) more training in domestic and international policy analysis. To initiate a global studies program, school districts and states should emphasize existing goals pertaining to citizenship education and global understanding and teachers should be involved in the planning and implementation of the process. Finally, the report outlines a scope and sequence of courses leading to global awareness by students and recommends appropriate materials for the courses. Appendices include a summary of recommendations of related reports, some statistical data on interdependence, an outline of the kinds of global education courses offered or required in selected states, a selected materials list, and a list of relevant curriculum development centers.

Task Force on International Education. *America In Transition: The International Frontier.* Washington, D.C.: National Governors' Association, 1989. ED number to be assigned. (Paper copy available only from the National Governors' Association, 444 N. Capitol, Suite 250, Washington, DC 20001, $10.95.)

More than ever, U.S. economic well-being is intertwined with that of other countries through expanding international trade, financial markets, and investments. National security, and even world stability, depend upon U.S. understanding of and communication with other countries. Therefore, international education must be an integral part of the education of every student. This report highlights individual examples of worthy international education programs at all levels from across the country. These pockets of progress must be nurtured and expanded until they grow into a national commitment to international education. State governors must take the lead in creating an international focus for the U.S. educational system at all levels. Critical to the success of this effort will be the involvement of a broad coalition including: teachers, school administrators and board members, legislators, university presidents, college faculty, and the business community. The following objectives for state action are recommended: (1) international education must become part of the basic education for all of students; (2) more students must gain proficiency in foreign languages; (3) teachers must know more about international issues; (4) schools and teachers must be aware of the wealth of resources and materials that are available for international education; (5) all college and university graduates must be knowledgeable about the broader world and conversant in another language; (6) business and community support of international education should be increased; and (7) the business community must have access to international education, particularly information about export markets, trade regulations, and overseas cultures. A 50-item bibliography is included.

Texas Education Agency. *Social Studies Framework: Kindergarten-Grade 12.* Austin: Texas Education Agency, 1986. ED 277 620.

This document provides general instructional guidelines for district administrators and teachers in Texas as they attempt to meet the goal of preparing students for citizenship in a democracy. The framework includes the legal requirements for social studies and provides guidelines to school districts in planning social studies programs for grades K through twelve. It reflects legislative mandates, State Board of Education rules, and developments in social studies education that have occurred since previous publications. It contains the following chapters: "Overview: The Social Studies Program, Kindergarten-Grade 12"; "Curriculum Documents"; "Aspects of the Social Studies Program"; "Social Studies Essential Elements"; and "Special Student Populations and the Social Studies." Appendices provide an outline of curriculum requirements prescribed by state law and state board of education rule; legislative provisions concerning experimental and local credit courses; legislative provisions concerning honors courses; and a set of suggested guidelines for evaluating social studies programs. A pull-out chart displays the social studies requirements for grades K through six.

Utah State Board of Education. *Elementary and Secondary Core Curriculum Standards. Social Studies: Level K-12.* Salt Lake City: Utah State Board of Education, 1987. ED 296 915.

This Utah State curriculum guide specifies social studies core curriculum standards that must be completed by all K-12 students in order to meet Utah graduation requirements. The core curriculum is intended to represent ideas, concepts, and skills that provide a basic social studies foundation upon which subsequent learnings may be built. An introductory section including the K-12 program of studies and graduation requirements statement considers: (1) educational philosophy; (2) elementary, middle, and high school policies and programs; (3) general requirements; and (4) social studies core curriculum goals. A general course description is provided for kindergarten through third grade and for fourth through sixth grade. Core course standards and accompanying objectives are included for each elementary grade level. Specific course titles, credit units, and prerequisites, along with course descriptions, standards, and objectives are provided for grades seven through twelve. A social studies course chart is included.

Walstad, William, and John C. Soper. *A Report Card on the Economic Literacy of U.S. High School Students.* New York: Joint Council on Economic Education, 1988. ED 310 055.

A study of over 3,000 U.S. high school students who took the Test of Economic Literacy (TEL) in 1986 reveals a lack of basic understanding in the four basic TEL concept clusters of fundamental economics, microeconomics, macroeconomics, and international economics. The TEL was administered pre- and posttest where students were enrolled in one of four types of courses: basic economics, "consumer economics," social studies with economics, and social studies without economics. Students in the economics courses did show significant improvement (+7.5 percent) after the TEL posttest examination while the others did not. Regression analysis was used to identify the effects of variables such as student background and environment or teacher and course preparation. Students in districts that participated in the Developmental Economic Education Program (DEEP) sponsored by the Joint Council on Economic Education scored higher than other students. The amount of college coursework in economics taken by the teachers themselves was directly related to increased student performance in the classroom. A significant amount of ignorance was displayed in basic concepts and relationships in macroeconomics and international economics. Three tables of TEL data and twelve references are included in the report.

John J. Patrick is Director of ERIC Clearinghouse for Social Studies/Social Science Education at Indiana University. C. Frederick Risinger is President of National Council for the Social Studies and Associate Director of ERIC.

Notes

Notes